15 Selected Units of English through the News Media

—2020 Edition—

Masami Takahashi

Noriko Itoh

Richard Powell

JN089218

Asahi Press

記事提供
The New York Times
The Japan Times
Bloomberg
Kyodo, AFP-Jiji

写真提供
アフロ：The New York Times／Redux／
Event Horizon Telescope／ZUMA Press／
Imaginechina／
ロイター／AP／Kyodo News／新華社

地図・イラスト
ヨシオカユリ

15 Selected Units of English through the News Media —2020 Edition—
Copyright © 2020 by Asahi Press

All rights reserved. No part of this book may be reproduced or transmitted in any form or by any means, electronic or mechanical, including photocopying, recording or by any information storage and retrieval system, without permission in writing from authors and the publisher.

は　し　が　き

　本書は、世界のニュースを通して Reading, Listening, Speaking, Writing のバランスのとれた学習が効果的にできるように工夫してあります。2018年10月：花崇拝を止めてコーランに、11月：iPS細胞を用いたパーキンソン病治療の臨床試験、2019年1月：高層アパート崩壊でロシアの背骨にひずみ；アフリカでの中国の優位性は貸付金のおかげ；なぜ第5世代携帯電話は安全ではないのか？、2月：ドイツ　高速道路で速度制限か？；イラン革命40周年で日常生活の支配が緩む；iPS細胞での脊髄損傷治療計画実施承認；ベネズエラから徒歩で脱出、3月：英語はもはや英米人だけのものではない、4月：日本の新元号は「令和」；フランス人　中国人によるぶどう園の名称変更に恐怖で縮み上がる；ブラックホールの初画像；国境での米国の恥；ケニアでは足が速いと身を滅ぼす；大統領にユダヤ人、心穏やかでないウクライナのユダヤ人、5月：男中心の日本社会は人口動態危機に直面　皇室も、まで世界中のニュースを満載しております。

　The New York Times, The New York Times International Edition, The Japan Times から社会・文化・政治経済・情報・言語・教育・科学・医学・環境・娯楽・スポーツなどのあらゆる分野を網羅しましたので、身近に世界中のニュースに触れ、読み、聞き、話し、書く楽しさを育みながら、多角的にそして複眼的に英語運用力が自然に培われるように意図しています。

　15課より構成され、各課に新聞記事読解前にBefore you readを設けました。本文の内容が予想できる写真と、どこにあるかを示す地図と国の情報を参照しながら自由に意見交換をします。次の Words and Phrases では、記事に記載されている単語や熟語とそれに合致する英語の説明を選び、あらかじめ大事な語の理解を深めて行きます。Summaryでは記事の内容を予想しながら、5語を適当な箇所に記入して要約文を完成させます。記事読解前では難しいようであれば、読解後に活用しても良いと思います。さらに、記事に関連した裏話も載せました。記事の読解にあたり、わかり易い註釈を記事の右端に付け、理解度をチェックするための Multiple Choice, True or False, 記事に関連した語法を学ぶVocabularyと豊富に取り揃えました。Summaryと記事がそのまま音声化されたファイルをウェブ上にあげています。多方面に渡る記事やExercisesを活用して、英字新聞に慣れ親しみ、使っていただけることを望んでいます。

　今回テキスト作成に際して、お世話になりました朝日出版社社長原雅久氏、編集部の日比野忠氏、小川洋一郎氏に心からお礼申し上げます。

2019年10月

高橋　優身

伊藤　典子

Richard Powell

CONTENTS

15 Selected Units of English through the News Media -2020 Edition-

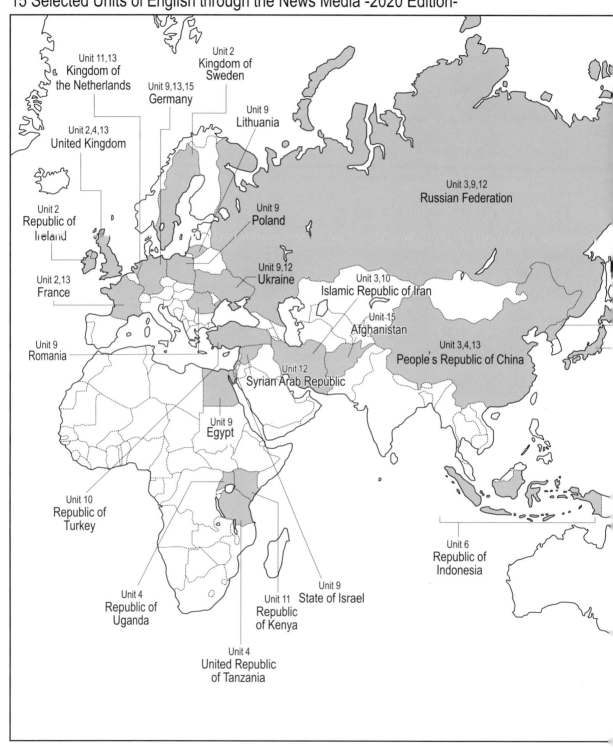

Unit 11,13
Kingdom of
the Netherlands

Unit 2
Kingdom of
Sweden

Unit 9,13,15
Germany

Unit 9
Lithuania

Unit 2,4,13
United Kingdom

Unit 3,9,12
Russian Federation

Unit 2
Republic of
Ireland

Unit 9
Poland

Unit 2,13
France

Unit 9,12
Ukraine

Unit 3,10
Islamic Republic of Iran

Unit 15
Afghanistan

Unit 9
Romania

Unit 3,4,13
People's Republic of China

Unit 12
Syrian Arab Republic

Unit 9
Egypt

Unit 10
Republic of
Turkey

Unit 6
Republic of
Indonesia

Unit 4
Republic of
Uganda

Unit 11
Republic
of Kenya

Unit 9
State of Israel

Unit 4
United Republic
of Tanzania

Unit 3
Democratic People's
Republic of Korea

Unit 1,5,15
Japan

Unit 2,3,4,8,13,14,15
U.S.A.

Unit 8
United Mexican
States

Unit 7
Bolivarian Republic
of Venezuela

Unit 7
Colombia

Unit 7
Ecuador

Unit 7
Peru

音声再生アプリ「リスニング・トレーナー」を使った音声ダウンロード

朝日出版社開発のアプリ、「リスニング・トレーナー（リストレ）」を使えば、教科書の音声をスマホ、タブレットに簡単にダウンロードできます。どうぞご活用ください。

◉ アプリ【リスニング・トレーナー】の使い方

《アプリのダウンロード》

App Store または Google Play から「リスニング・トレーナー」のアプリ（無料）をダウンロード

App Storeはこちら▶

Google Playはこちら▶

《アプリの使い方》

① アプリを開き「コンテンツを追加」をタップ
② 画面上部に【15655】を入力しDoneをタップ

音声ストリーミング配信 》》》

この教科書の音声は、右記ウェブサイトにて無料で配信しています。

https://text.asahipress.com/free/english/

15 Selected Units of
English through the News Media

Unit 1

- 日本の新元号は「令和」
- 男中心の日本社会は人口動態危機に直面 皇室も

新元号を発表する菅官房長官　　　Photo: Kyodo News

Before you read

Japan　日本国

面積　377,961.73km²
人口　126,530,000人
　　　日本民族　98.5%
　　　朝鮮人　0.5%
　　　中国人　0.4%
首都　東京都
最大都市　大阪市　（昼間人口）
　　　　　横浜市　（夜間人口）
　　　　　東京都23区部
GDP　4兆9,386億ドル（世界３位）
公用語　なし、事実上日本語
宗教　無宗教信者　52%
　　　仏教　35%　/ 神道　4％
　　　キリスト教　2.3%
政治　立憲君主制
識字率　99.8%

次の１～５の語の説明として最も近いものをａ～ｅから１つ選び、（　　）内に記入しなさい。

1. herald 　　　　　（　　）　　a. start
2. initiate 　　　　（　　）　　b. based on the usual meaning
3. compilation 　　（　　）　　c. decline in number or power
4. literally 　　　　（　　）　　d. signal or report
5. dwindle 　　　　（　　）　　e. collection

Summary

次の英文は記事の要約です。下の語群から最も適切な語を１つ選び、（　　）内に記入しなさい。

02

Japanese people had to wait until one month before the new Reiwa Era
(　　　　　) to learn its name. Some were (　　　　　) by the word "rei",
which may mean "command" as well as "auspicious". At the ceremony to
(　　　　　) the new emperor the small number of heirs was (　　　　　),
as was the (　　　　　) that they are all male.

commenced　　confused　　fact　　install　　striking

　平成31年４月30日平成天皇陛下が退位され、翌日令和元年５月１日０時徳仁天皇陛下が、第126代天皇に即位された。新天皇陛下は、皇位継承に伴う最初の儀式「剣璽等承継の儀」に臨み、皇位の証しとして剣と勾玉などを受け継がれた。その後、「即位後朝見の儀」で「国民に寄り添い、憲法にのっとり象徴としての責務を果たす」と天皇として初のお言葉を述べられた。

　元号も平成から令和に改められた。日本最古の歌集「万葉集」の「梅花の歌32首」の序文が「令和」の出典となった。序文は703年に32首が詠まれ、「初春の令月にして、気淑く風和らぎ、梅は鏡前の粉を披き、蘭は珮後の香を薫す」が「令和」の典拠となった。中西進さんの現代語訳は、「新春の好き月、空気は美しく風は和かに、梅は美女の鏡の前に装う白粉のごとく白く咲き、蘭は身を飾った香の如きかおりを漂わせている」となっている。

　外務省は、「令和」を英訳「beautiful harmony（美しい調和）」と決めた。つまり、美しく麗しき和を築くことである。

Reading

03

Japan's next era to be named Reiwa

| Eagerly awaited name revealed one month before new era is set to begin, at start of May 1 |

In a much-awaited moment that heralded the approach of a new chapter in Japan's history, Chief Cabinet Secretary Yoshihide Suga announced Monday that the new Imperial era will be named Reiwa, in one of the final steps toward initiating
5 the nation's first Imperial succession in three decades.

Holding up a placard that displayed the kanji characters for the new era, Suga said the name was formulated based on the introduction to a set of poems from "Manyoshu," the oldest existing compilation of Japanese poetry. The first character
10 represents "good fortune," while the second can be translated as "peace" or "harmony."

04

The arrival of the Reiwa Era will in turn end the 30-year run of the Heisei ("achieving peace") Era, which began in Jan. 8, 1989.

15 Later on Monday, Prime Minister Shinzo Abe told a news conference that the government chose the kanji characters because they signify "a culture being born and nurtured by people coming together beautifully."

The naming of a new Imperial era is a significant event
20 here, with such names playing an integral role, both practically and psychologically, in the lives of Japanese people.

05

Local municipality officials, computer engineers and calendar manufacturers, for example, have spent months preparing for the various adjustments involved.

25 Many Japanese people are not familiar with use of "rei" to mean "good fortune" or "auspicious." For most, the first phrase that comes to mind is likely to be "meirei," which literally means an order or command from a supervisor.

The Japan Times, April 2, 2019

era：元号

revealed：《ヘッドラインの場合、受動態は be 動詞を省略する》
at start of ～：～の開始と同時に

Chief Cabinet Secretary：内閣官房長官

first Imperial succession in three decades：前回から30年ぶりの皇位継承

a culture … beautifully：人々が美しい心を寄せ合う中で、文化が生まれ育つ

here：日本では
integral：不可欠な

municipality：地方自治体

involved：関連する《名詞を後ろから修飾する》

auspicious：幸先の良い

Patriarchal Japan Faces a Demographic Crisis. And So Do Its Royals.

TOKYO — It looked a little lonely up there.

During the short, solemn ceremony on Wednesday in which the new emperor of Japan, Naruhito, 59, accepted the sacred sword, jewels and seals that signify his right to sit on the throne, he was flanked by just two people. Standing ramrod straight to his right was his younger brother, Prince Akishino. To his left was his aging uncle, Prince Hitachi, who sat in a wheelchair.

It was striking visual evidence of the imperial family's looming existential crisis: It has precious few heirs left.

Like Japan itself, the imperial family has a demographic problem. Just as Japan's population is shrinking and aging, so is the royal family's. The line of succession, which is limited to men, is only three people long.

Under rules set by a government committee, only adult male members of the royal family were permitted to witness the rites.

Prime Minister Shinzo Abe has pushed a platform of elevating women in the often patriarchal Japanese workplace, hoping to supplement the country's dwindling labor force and energize its economy.

Similarly, the imperial family may have to consider permitting women to join the line succession.

The New York Times International Edition, May 2, 2019

Patriarchal：男中心の
Demographic：人口動態の

up there：皇室で進行中

short：簡潔な（数が足りないとの意味もある）
accepted：《日本国憲法下の皇位継承儀式では、「剣璽等承継の儀」として皇位の証しである剣璽（剣と勾玉）と共に国璽と御璽の承継が行われる》
seals：国璽と御璽《国家の表徴として押す璽（印章または印影）、外交文書などの国家の重要文書に押される：国璽は国家の印章で御璽は天皇の印章》
throne：帝位
Standing … was：《倒置》
ramrod straight：背筋を伸ばして
Prince Akishino：秋篠宮皇嗣殿下
Prince Hitachi：常陸宮殿下
visual evidence：物的証拠
existential crisis：実存的危機
precious few：極めて少数の
heirs：継承者
line of succession：継承順位
platform：政策

dwindling：減少している

energize ～：～を活性化させる

Exercises

次の１～５の英文を完成させるために、 ａ～ｄの中から最も適切なものを１つ選びなさい。

1. The name of the outgoing era in Japan is
    a. Showa Era.
    b. Meiji Era.
    c. Reiwa Era.
    d. Heisei Era.

2. Japan's new era is
    a. the first new era in 36 years.
    b. the first in 30 decades.
    c. the first in 3 decades.
    d. the first in 13 decades.

3. The word "rei"
    a. has only one meaning to the average citizen.
    b. is part of the new era and can have several different meanings.
    c. has no prior meaning for the citizens.
    d. provides for the future.

4. A problem evident from the ceremonies is that
    a. there are too few males on the horizon for future needs.
    b. female members want to ascend to the throne.
    c. there are too many males to ascend to the throne.
    d. Prime Minister Abe is against female rulers.

5. The Reiwa Era will last
    a. for three decades.
    b. as long as Emperor Naruhito reigns.
    c. until the aging population has ceased to exist.
    d. until women are permitted to attend the ceremonies.

True or False

本文の内容に合致するものに T（True）、合致しないものに F（False）をつけなさい。

( ) **1.** The royals' male population is abundant.

( ) **2.** Females in Japan attended the ceremony for the first time this year.

( ) **3.** Prince Akishino was allowed to view the ceremony for his brother.

( ) **4.** Preparing for the new Era required the efforts of many different officials in the government.

( ) **5.** The characters to write Reiwa were inspired by the Manyoshu poetry.

Vocabulary

次の英文は、The Japan Times に掲載された *Emperor Naruhito's reign begins*『徳仁天皇陛下即位』の記事の一部です。下の語群から最も適切なものを１つ選び、（　　）内に記入しなさい。

Born after World War II, the 59-year-old became the (　　　) of the state overnight.　Under Japan's postwar Constitution, the emperor is (　　　) from exercising political power.

The (　　　) put an end to the 30-year run of the Heisei (Achieving Peace) imperial era, in turn ushering in a new era called Reiwa (Beautiful Harmony) at midnight – a moment marked by nationwide celebrations.

In this ceremony, chamberlains were seen carrying a (　　　) and a jewel — two of the three (　　　) treasures of the imperial family — as well as the state and privy seals before placing them on tables, in a gesture acknowledging his (　　　) and the inheritance of the regalia and seals.

At the start of his speech, the new monarch said he is "filled with a sense of (　　　)" as he thinks about the heavy (　　　) he was undertaking with his new role.

abdication	barred	responsibility	sacred
solemnity	succession	sword	symbol

●英語はもはや英米人だけのものではない

英国の EU 離脱により英国民の将来はどうなるのか　Photo: ロイター／アフロ

Before you read

英語が公用語の国：

United Kingdom, Ireland, United States of America, Canada, Australia, New Zealand, Antigua and Barbuda, Bahamas, Barbados, Belize, Botswana, Cameroon, Cook Islands, Dominica, Eritrea, Eswatini, Fiji, Gambia, Ghana, Grenada, Guyana, India, Jamaica, Kenya, Kiribati, Lesotho, Liberia, Malawi, Malta, Marshall Islands, Mauritius, Micronesia, Namibia, Nauru, Nigeria, Niue, Pakistan, Palau, Papua New Guinea, Philippines, Rwanda, Saint Christopher and Nevis, Saint Lucia, Saint Vincent and the Grenadines, Samoa, Seychelles, Sierra Leone, Singapore, Solomon Islands, Somaliland, South Africa, South Sudan, Sudan, Tanzania, Tonga, Trinidad and Tobago, Tuvalu, Uganda, Vanuatu, Zambia, Zimbabwe

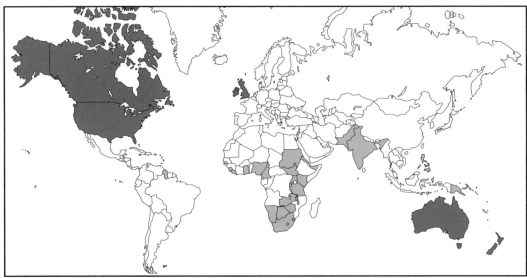

次の１～５の語の説明として最も近いものを a～e から１つ選び、(　　)内に記入しなさい。

1. apprehension　　(　　)　　**a.** keep
2. domain　　　　 (　　)　　**b.** fear
3. bloc　　　　　 (　　)　　**c.** institution
4. body　　　　　 (　　)　　**d.** group
5. retain　　　　 (　　)　　**e.** home country or area

Summary

次の英文は記事の要約です。下の語群から最も適切な語を１つ選び、(　　) 内に記入しなさい。

08

The global expansion of English has (　　　　　) advantages to countries where it is spoken natively. But despite American (　　　　　) from many international organizations, and UK (　　　　　) to leave the EU, the language continues to grow. Most speakers are now (　　　　　), so the link between English and Anglo-Saxon culture is (　　　　　).

attempts　　brought　　nonnative　　weakening　　withdrawal

世界人口70億人のうち、英語人口が約17億5000万人いると言われている。４人に１人、世界総人口の25% もいる。しかし、17.5億人のうち英語 native speaker は、3.79億人しかいず、残りの13.7億人は英語を第二言語として使用している。

標準中国語の native speaker・第二言語話者数が10.51億人もいるが、英語は、世界で最も使用されている言語である。地理的・経済力・コミュニケーション力・メディア力・外交力から見ても英語が最強の言語とされている。ここに英語の重要性と必要性が明らかである。

英語 non-native speaker よって話され、使われている英語を複数形 World Englishes と言われ、各話者の国の文化や言語的背景が表されている。英語 native speaker には、World Englishes は間違いであるとか、あるいは non-native speaker の中にも native 至上主義の考え方を持った人たちが主流である。しかし、ビジネスの世界でも native speaker よりも non-native speaker と英語を使って取引きをする方が圧倒的に多い。もちろん正しい英語ときれいな発音で話すことが大切だが、コミュニケーション能力、つまり相手にいかに伝え、相手をいかに理解するかの方がもっと重要である。

Reading

09

Brits and Americans no longer own English

The Brexit circus and the unpopularity of U.S. President Donald Trump are causing apprehension about the future of the Anglosphere, the cultural, intellectual and political influence of the core English-speaking nations: Britain and
5 the United States.

As a non-native English speaker who works in the Anglosphere, though, I'm not worried about that; Americans and Brits are merely facing increasing competition from within their accustomed domain rather than from without.

10

10 The English language, which has just 379 million native speakers, is spoken at a useful level by some 1.7 billion people, according to the British Council. That has long ensured that U.S. and U.K. voices are heard louder than any others.

There is no indication that the language's popularity is
15 declining despite the recent damage to the two countries' soft power. Last year, the British Council forecast that the number of potential learners in Europe will decline by 8.8 percent, or some 15.3 million, between 2015 and 2025. Brexit has nothing to do with this: The expansion of English teaching at schools
20 is expected to cut demand for the organization's courses. Overall, the market for English in education is predicted to grow by 17 percent a year to reach $22 billion in 2024.

11

It's impossible to avoid: 54 percent of all websites are in it. The global academic community speaks it, and not just
25 because U.S. and U.K. universities are important: If they all closed tomorrow, scholars would still need a common tongue, and they aren't going to vote to adopt another one.

Nor will the global political community. The European Union is a case in point: After Brexit, English could lose
30 the status as one of the bloc's working languages because no remaining members use it officially. Yet the legal departments of all the EU governing bodies have agreed that it can retain

---

Brits：イギリス人

Brexit：英国の EU 離脱
circus：大騒ぎ、大混乱
apprehension：不安、心配
Anglosphere：アングロスフィア《英語圏のうち、自由や権利を保障する英米の基本法を支持し、同質の価値観や文化を形成している国々》

accustomed domain：いつもの領域

British Council：英国文化振興会

indication that ～：～を示す徴候
soft power：ソフト・パワー《（軍事力ではなく）他国の心情的援助・共感などを背景に他国を味方に付ける（国の）力》

important：有力な

European Union：欧州連合（EU）
case in point：好適例
working languages：使用言語
legal departments：法務部門
governing bodies：運営組織

its status on the rather thin argument that it's used in Irish and Maltese law. Even after Brexit, it will share with German the status of the most widely spoken language in the EU — that is, as long as one takes into account non-native speakers.

The EU's post-Brexit experiment will be important for the Anglosphere's future. A large bureaucracy and an entire political establishment will be setting the agenda in English, but without the participation of native speakers. As Marko Modiano of the University of Gavle in Sweden wrote in a recent paper (in English, of course): "When using English, EU citizens will all be on the same footing, that is to say, they will be communicating in a second language, and as such, only a relatively small number of people will have an unfair advantage."

When the U.S. quit UNESCO, the United Nations' culture and science organization, earlier this year, English remained the lingua franca of the Paris-based organization that has long sought to push back against its dominance.

Native speakers still get something of an unfair advantage when it comes to that, of course. But it is no longer inextricably linked to power, hard or soft.

The Japan Times, March 9, 2019

---

on the argument that ～ : ～という理由で
Maltese : マルタ島の

takes into account ～ : ～を考慮する

political establishment : 政治的既成勢力
agenda : 会議事項

University of Gavle : イェヴレ大学《1977年設立》
paper : 学術論文

on the same footing : 同じ条件で、対等で
as such : したがって

UNESCO : 国際連合教育科学文化機関（ユネスコ）

lingua franca : 共通語

push back against ～ : ～に反対する
get something of ～ : ～で得をする
when it comes to ～ : ～に関して言えば
power, hard : ハード・パワー《軍事力や経済力による威嚇などを背景にした（国の）力》

Exercises

Multiple Choice

次の１の英文の質問に答え、２〜５の英文を完成させるために、 a 〜 d の中から最も適切なものを１つ選びなさい。

1. How many native speakers of English are there now?

   a. 15.3 million people.

   b. 1.7 billion people.

   c. 379 million people.

   d. 17% of the world's population.

2. After the U.S. withdrawal from UNESCO, the French

   a. demanded to become the dominant language.

   b. continued to speak in English.

   c. decided to withdraw from UNESCO.

   d. kept Chinese as an official language.

3. EU citizens using English as a second language

   a. are at disadvantage with native speakers, but not with each other.

   b. gained the power that Britain and the U.S. used to possess.

   c. realize that German is as popular a language as English.

   d. are uncomfortable speaking in it.

4. Academics and scholars have chosen _____ for communication.

   a. German

   b. Gaelic

   c. English

   d. Italian

5. In the future, the European political experiment will

   a. stop setting the agenda in English.

   b. require more native language speakers as interpreters.

   c. continue setting the agenda in English.

   d. turn into an overwhelming agenda of confusion.

本文の内容に合致するものにＴ（True）、合致しないものにＦ（False）をつけなさい。

(   ) **1.** English and German are equally popular as the common language of the EU.

(   ) **2.** As the influence of the U.S. and Britain declines, the popularity of English as a main language will also change.

(   ) **3.** This article does not mention what is the most common language of websites.

(   ) **4.** The educational market for English will grow 17% a year.

(   ) **5.** English is a powerful language that dominates business.

Vocabulary

次の１〜７は、「language」に関する英文です。日本文に合わせて（   ）内に最も適切な語を下の語群から１つ選び、記入しなさい。

1. 言語とは、月による潮の満ち引きのように隠れた力を引き出すものである。
Language exerts (   ) power, like the moon on the tides.

2. 言語は、使う人々に知的財産を与えている。
Language embodies the (   ) wealth of the people who use it.

3. １つの言語が分かるとあなたの人生に１つの廊下が現れる。２つの言語が分かると、その廊下にあるあらゆる扉が開く。
One language sets you in a corridor for life. Two languages open every (   ) along the way.

4. 言語は、魂の血液である。思想はその血液へ流し込まれ、その血液の中で育つ。
Language is the blood of the soul where (   ) are absorbed and nurtured.

5. 言語は文化の道しるべである。その言語を話す人間がどこから来て、どこに向かっているのかを教えてくれる。
Language is the road map of a culture. It (   ) you where its people come from and where they are going.

6. 外国語について何も知らないものは、自国語についても何も知らない。
Those who know nothing of foreign languages know nothing of their (   ).

7. 相手が理解できる言語で話すと、言葉は相手の頭に届く。相手の母国語で話すと言葉は相手の心に届く。
If you talk to a man in a language he understands, that goes to his head. If you talk to him in his language, that goes to his (   ).

> door   heart   hidden   intellectual   own   tells   thoughts

Unit **3**

● なぜ第５世代携帯電話は安全ではないのか？

中国モバイル上海支店の５G広告

Photo: Imaginechina／アフロ

Before you read

1. What do you think the article will be about?

    この記事は何の話題についてだと思いますか？

2. How insecure do you think 5G is?

    第５世代がどのように安全でないと思いますか？

次の１〜５の語の説明として最も近いものを a〜e から１つ選び、（　　）内に記入しなさい。

1.	vulnerable	（　　）	**a.**	life-changing
2.	envision	（　　）	**b.**	at risk
3.	transformational	（　　）	**c.**	able to control itself
4.	backbone	（　　）	**d.**	spine, or main support
5.	autonomous	（　　）	**e.**	foresee or conceive

Summary

次の英文は記事の要約です。下の語群から最も適切な語を１つ選び、（　　）内に記入しなさい。

14

5G networks are much faster than the 4G (　　　　　) we use today. By speeding up data input from (　　　　　) sources they will enhance the technology needed for autonomous cars. But technical advances come with (　　　　　). If 5G is hacked, the (　　　　　) could be extreme. We need to make it (　　　　　), so that driving and medical surgery will be safe.

> consequences　　multiple　　ones　　risks　　secure

　　5G の G は "Generation" を表す。1990年代初頭に1G が開始され、携帯機器間でメールを受信・返信することを可能にし、それが2G に拡大して行った。世界は、さらに3G に移動し、人々は電話をかけたり、メールを送ったり、インターネットを閲覧したり、検索したりすることができた。

　　4G は、ワイヤレスの第３世代で可能になった機能の多くを強化した。使用者は、net を検索・閲覧したり、メールを受信・送信したり、電話を受けたり・かけたりすることができ、大きなビデオファイルを簡単にダウンロードしてアップロードすることができた。その後、LTE（Long Term Evolution）長期にわたる進化を追加して、4G に接続した。

　　5G は、毎秒最大10ギガビットのダウンロード速度を増加し、使用者がメールの送信、電話をかけたり、net を常に閲覧したりできるように、network 経由でデータが転送される速度がさらに向上する。スマートフォン、時計、自動車、家電製品、防犯カメラ、犬の首輪、ドアロックなどには、Internet 接続が益々求められている。

　　4G より5G の方が通信速度が数10倍から100倍速いし、回線につながる状態が安定し、色々な機器に net を繋げることができる。2020年の東京オリンピックでは5G の開始を目標にしている。

Reading

15

Why isn't 5G secure?

5G：第5世代移動通信システム

    The Trump administration's so-called "race" with China to build new fifth-generation (5G) wireless networks is speeding toward a network vulnerable to Chinese (and other) cyberattacks. So far, the Trump administration has focused on 5 blocking Chinese companies from being a part of the network, but these efforts are far from sufficient.

toward ～：～に関して
vulnerable to ～：～に対して弱い
blocking ～ from …：～が…するのを阻止する

16

    Our current wireless networks are fourth-generation, or 4G. It was 4G that gave us the smartphone. Reaching the next level of mobile services, however, requires increased speed 10 on the network. Fifth-generation networks are designed to be 10 to 100 times faster than today's typical wireless connection with much lower latency (response time). These speeds will open up all kinds of new functional possibilities. Those new functions, in turn, will attract cyberintrusions just like honey 15 attracts a bear.

It was 4G that ～：《強調構文》
lower latency：低遅延の、待ち時間が長い
cyberintrusions：サイバー侵入

    Some envision 5G as a kind of "wireless fiber" for the delivery of television and internet much like a cable system does today. Iranians hacking the delivery of "Game of Thrones" isn't good, but the real transformational promise of 20 5G goes far beyond wireless cable and its security is much more critical.

envision ～ as …：～を…と思い描く
hacking ～：～をハッキングする《コンピュータ・システムに不法侵入する》
"Game of Thrones"：『ゲーム・オブ・スローンズ』《ファンタジー小説シリーズ『氷と炎の歌』を原作としたテレビドラマシリーズ》
promise：見込み
critical：危機的な

17

    The most exciting part of the 5G future is how its speed will change the very nature of the internet. Thus far, the internet has been all about transporting data from point A to point B. 25 Today's internet-connected car may be able to get driving directions sent to it, but it is essentially the same as getting email: the one-way transportation of pre-existing information. The autonomous car is something vastly different, in which the 5G network allows computers to orchestrate a flood of 30 information from multitudes of input sensors for real time, on-the-fly decision-making. It is estimated that the data output of a single autonomous vehicle in one day will be equal to

very nature：性質（本性）そのもの
all about ～：要は～だ
get driving directions：駆動方向、ナビ［道案内］を受け取る
orchestrate ～：～を統合する
input sensors：センサー入力
on-the-fly decision making：即断即決で

today's daily data output of three thousand people.

18

35　　Leadership in 5G technology is not just about building a network, but also about whether that network will be secure enough for the innovations it promises. And the 5G "race" is more complex and dangerous than industry and the Trump administration portray. When 5G enables autonomous vehicles, do we want those cars and trucks crashing into each
40 other because the Russians hacked the network? If 5G will be the backbone of breakthroughs such as remote surgery, should that network be vulnerable to the North Koreans breaking into a surgical procedure?

19

　　As the President's National Security Telecommunications
45 Advisory Committee told him in November, "the cybersecurity threat now poses an existential threat to the future of the Nation."

　　Worse than ignoring the warnings, the Trump administration has repealed existing protections. Shortly
50 after taking office, the Trump F.C.C. removed a requirement imposed by the Obama F.C.C. that the 5G technical standard must be designed from the outset to withstand cyberattacks.

　　The Trump administration has been told that cybersecurity is an "existential risk." The new Congress should use its
55 oversight power to explore just why the administration has failed to protect against that risk, especially when it comes to the next generation of networks.

The New York Times International Edition, January 24, 2019

innovations：技術革新

industry：産業界

breakthroughs：飛躍的進歩

President's National … Committee：大統領直属の国家安全保障電気通信諮問委員会

cybersecurity threat：サイバー・セキュリティー《インターネットなどのサイバースペースにおいて、システムの破壊、不正侵入、情報の流出、データの改竄などから保護するための対策》に対する脅威

poses a threat to 〜：〜に脅威を与える

repealed 〜：〜を無効にした

taking office：（大統領）就任

F.C.C.：米国連邦通信委員会

requirement：要求

technical standard：技術規格

from the outset：最初から

withstand 〜：〜に耐える

oversight power：監視する法的権限

Exercises

Multiple Choice

次の1～5の英文を完成させるために、a～dの中から最も適切なものを1つ選びなさい。

1. This article compares the power of 5G to
   - **a.** an automobile.
   - **b.** an orchestra.
   - **c.** a one-way transportation system.
   - **d.** a complex information network.

2. The rapidity of 5G promises to
   - **a.** deliver information 10 to 100 times faster than today's wireless connections.
   - **b.** enhance the capability of autonomous cars.
   - **c.** change the nature of the internet.
   - **d.** achieve all of the above possibilities.

3. It cannot be said that
   - **a.** it is necessary to make the new network secure.
   - **b.** there is a danger of other countries hacking the system.
   - **c.** there are few security problems surrounding 5G.
   - **d.** surgical operations might be endangered by cyberattack.

4. Mr. Trump
   - **a.** was overly aware of the need to protect against cybercriminals.
   - **b.** ignored advice and repealed security measures for the system.
   - **c.** retained the security policy adopted by Obama.
   - **d.** reacted to security concerns in all of the above ways.

5. The most important benefit of the 5G system will be
   - **a.** watching cable TV on a faster system.
   - **b.** the lack of worry about cyber security.
   - **c.** higher speeds transforming the nature of the internet.
   - **d.** making Trump's political position more secure.

本文の内容に合致するものに T（True）、合致しないものに F（False）をつけなさい。

(   ) **1.** Mr. Trump is attempting to block Chinese companies from being a part of the new network but his efforts are not enough.

(   ) **2.** We should protect the 5G system only from China and need not worry about other countries.

(   ) **3.** An autonomous car fitted with 5G can do the work of 3,000 persons.

(   ) **4.** The writer thinks Congress should not interfere with cyber security policy.

(   ) **5.** Current smartphone technology is powered by a 3G network.

Vocabulary

次の英文は、Internet に掲載された *What Is 5G and How Will It Make My Life Better* 『5G とは何か、そしてどのように私の生活をより良くするのか？』の投稿の一部です。下の語群から最も適切なものを１つ選び、（   ）内に記入しなさい。

Everybody loves speedy internet, so it's no surprise that every major telecom in the world is working to make it even (   ). Smartphones, watches, homes, and cars are increasingly (   ) stable internet connections. In order to pipe in enough bandwidth for that precious wireless feed, we're going to need an entirely (   ) form of wireless signal – that's where 5G comes in.

Similar to 4G and 3G before it, 5G is a wireless connection built specifically to keep (   ) with the proliferation of devices that need a mobile internet connection. It's not just your phone and your computer anymore, either. Home (   ), door locks, security cameras, cars, wearables, dog collars, and so many other inert devices are beginning to connect to the web.

5G's speeds will be significantly faster. Currently, 4G LTE transfer speeds top out at about one gigabite per second. That means it (   ) about an hour to download a short HD movie in perfect conditions. The problem is, people rarely experience 4G's maximum download speed because the signal can be (   ) by so many different things: buildings, microwaves, other wifi signals.

appliances	disrupted	faster	new
requiring	takes	up	

●アフリカにおける中国の優位性は貸付金のおかげ

中国・ウガンダ産業博覧会。ウガンダ国民の将来がよくなれば…
Photo: 新華社／アフロ

Before you read

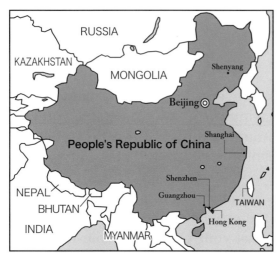

People's Republic of China
中華人民共和国

面積	9,634,057km² （日本の約25.5倍）
人口	1,374,620,000人（世界1位）
首都	北京 ／ 最大都市 上海
公用語	中国語 ／ 識字率 95.9%
民族	漢族 11億7000万～12億人（90%～92%）
	55の少数民族8% チワン族（1600万人）
	満族（1000万人） 回族（900万人）
	ミャオ族（800万人） ウイグル族・イ族（各700万人） ブイ族（300万人）
宗教	宗教信者 1億人 8%
	仏教 6.2% ／ キリスト教 2.3%
	道教・民俗宗教 87.4% ／ イスラム教 1.7%
GDP	11兆2182億ドル（世界2位） ／ 通貨 元
政体	一党独裁制の社会主義共和国

Republic of Uganda ウガンダ共和国
1962年に英国より独立、英連邦加盟国

面積	241,000km²（日本の本州とほぼ同じ）
人口	42,860,000人 首都 カンパラ
公用語	英語・スワヒリ語 ／ 識字率 73%
民族	バガンダ族、ランゴ族、アチョリ族
宗教	キリスト教 60% ／ 伝統宗教 30%
	イスラム教 10%
GDP	259億ドル ／ 通貨 ウガンダシリング
政体	共和制

次の１〜５の語の説明として最も近いものをa〜eから１つ選び、（　　）内に記入しなさい。

1. edge　　　　　　（　　）　　a. aggressive
2. predatory　　　（　　）　　b. compete
3. plunder　　　　（　　）　　c. advantage
4. consortium　　（　　）　　d. group collaborating together
5. jockey　　　　　（　　）　　e. steal

Summary

次の英文は記事の要約です。下の語群から最も適切な語を１つ選び、（　　）内に記入しなさい。

20

China has long (　　　　　　　) an aggressive economic policy in Africa. Some people fear it has military (　　　　　　). And many think it results in (　　　　　　) countries getting into heavy debt. But one American group recently (　　　　　　) its Chinese rivals for an oil refinery contract. They succeeded by offering the Africans a 40% (　　　　　　) in the project.

objectives　　outbid　　pursued　　recipient　　stake

2013年に習近平国家主席が、ヨーロッパとアジアを繋ぐ「一帯（シルクロード経済ベルト）」と南シナ海やインド洋を繋ぐ「一路（21世紀海上シルクロード）」の構築を提案した。この２つの経済圏構想を合わせて「一帯一路」と呼ばれるようになった。この沿線国は65か国あるが、100以上の国と国際組織の支持を得ている。

　沿線国間とは、政策交流、インフラ相互連結、貿易推進、資金融通、国民交流の５つを柱に掲げている。

　「一帯一路」攻勢は、アジア・ヨーロッパだけでなく、南米、アフリカへも及んでいる。2019年３月には、イタリアと「一帯一路」の協力に関する覚書に署名を交わした。地中海とヨーロッパ諸国を結ぶトリエステ港の開発など約3,100億円規模の経済協力を進めることになった。中・東欧16か国とも協力関係を築いている。

　さらに中国のアフリカ重視も際立っている。国連などで投票権のあるアフリカ54か国の支持に重きを置き、資源や市場確保だけでなく、自国主導の新たな国際秩序構築を目指している。しかし、中国の野心と新興国を借金漬けにしている「debt trap 借金地獄」の批判は避けられることができない。

Reading

21

China's edge in Africa: Loans

U.S. condemns 'debt trap' that is making it harder for its contractors to compete

China's investments in Africa are central to President Xi Jinping's signature Belt and Road Initiative, a trillion-dollar program to build infrastructure and extend Beijing's influence around the globe.

5　　The Trump administration has accused China of engaging in predatory lending aimed at trapping countries in debt, acquiring strategic assets like ports, and spreading corruption and authoritarian values. In response, the United States has announced an effort to help American businesses compete.

22

10　　The idea is to challenge China's infrastructure program while also pushing back against its trade practices, cybertheft and expanding military facilities and presence in the Pacific and Indian Oceans.

　　In Africa, American businesses have been largely absent 15　while Chinese companies have put down roots, nurturing powerful allies through both legitimate and illegal means.

　　The African Great Lakes have long tempted outsiders seeking riches, including the European nations that began plundering the continent in the 19th century. But in 2006, 20　four decades after the end of British rule in Uganda, a prize untapped by the colonialists was discovered: oil deposits by Lake Albert that are among the largest in East Africa, enough to transform parts of impoverished Uganda.

23

25　　Mr. Museveni's government negotiated for years with foreign companies before agreeing to a plan for extraction and the construction of a pipeline southeast to the Tanzanian coast, where the oil could be shipped around the world.

　　But Mr. Museveni also insisted on building a refinery in Uganda to ease the region's dependence on imported fuel.

30　　Uganda received more than 40 proposals to build the

edge：優位性、出発点
Loans：貸付金
'debt trap'：「借金地獄」
contractors：請負業者

President Xi Jinping：習近平国家主席
signature：特徴的な
Belt and Road Initiative：「一路一帯」《経済圏構想》
Beijing：北京

predatory lending：略奪的な貸付
strategic assets：戦略兵器
authoritarian values：独裁的な価値観

presence：軍隊の駐留、存在感

allies：同盟
legitimate：合法的な

untapped：未だ開発されなかった

refinery：精油所

refinery.

Leading one bid was Dongsong, a private hydropower and mining company in the southern Chinese city of Guangzhou.
A proposal made outside formal channels came from the
35 China National Offshore Oil Corporation, or CNOOC, the country's third-largest state oil company.

24

Both companies had offices in Kampala, the capital of Uganda, and had worked closely for years with the Ministry of Energy and Mineral Development.

40 But their proposals included tough terms, according to interviews and an internal government assessment reviewed by The Times.

Dongsong wanted a sovereign loan guarantee — making the Ugandan government responsible for the project's debt if
45 it failed — and insisted that 60 percent of labor and materials come from China. CNOOC, meanwhile, wanted greater access to the oil fields themselves.

25

The American consortium tried to set itself apart, proposing that Uganda's state oil company and other East African nations
50 own up to 40 percent of a new private company that would build and run the refinery.

The consortium would finance the project by selling shares to investors as well as by borrowing, but it was not asking for a sovereign guarantee.

55 In Uganda, all major decisions end up before Mr. Museveni. Officials jockey for his ear, and the president is adept at playing them off one another.

That gave the Americans an opening.

The New York Times, January 14, 2019

Leading one bid was Dongsong：《過去進行形の倒置 Dongsong が主語》
bid：立候補団体
Dongsong：東方
Guangzhou：広州
China National Offshore Oil Corporation：中国海洋石油集団《国有石油・天然ガス会社》

Ministry of Energy and Mineral Development：エネルギー鉱物省

terms：条件

The Times：タイムズ《英国で1785年に創刊した世界最古の日刊新聞》
loan guarantee：借入保証

access to ～：～を利用できる権利
consortium：合弁企業、共同体
set itself apart：際立つようにする

finance ～：～に資金融資する
shares：株

end up ～：結局～となる
jockey for his ear：耳に入れようと争う
adept at ～：～が上手だ
playing ～ off：～が争うように仕向ける
opening：機会、チャンス

Exercises

次の１〜５の英文を完成させるために、ａ〜ｄの中から最も適切なものを１つ選びなさい。

1. The U.S. is working to
   a. receive a good price on the oil from Uganda.
   b. praise China for bringing Uganda into debt.
   c. allow fair competition for its contractors in Uganda.
   d. honor China with debt.

2. According to the U.S., China's operating policies allow for
   a. trade practices that are unfair to Uganda.
   b. Chinese cybertheft in Uganda.
   c. the expansion of military facilities in the region.
   d. all of the above Chinese actions.

3. The natural resource that brought attention to Uganda was
   a. the beautiful jungle vegetation.
   b. the oil discovered near Lake Albert.
   c. a new pipeline to Tanzania.
   d. labor and resources from China.

4. Dongsong made a proposal for a refinery that
   a. would leave Uganda owing money to China if the pipeline failed.
   b. sought greater access to the oil fields.
   c. required 40% of the labor coming from China, not Uganda.
   d. involved all of the above demands.

5. The long time president of Uganda
   a. will not weigh information about what will be best for his country.
   b. leans towards accepting China's assistance.
   c. is willing to listen to all proposals for the right refinery project.
   d. is a good friend of President Xi Jinping.

本文の内容に合致するものに T (True)、合致しないものに F (False) をつけなさい。

(   )   **1.**   The oil deposits in Lake Albert are among the largest in East Africa.

(   )   **2.**   Mr. Museveni is the President of Uganda.

(   )   **3.**   The writer feels it is fair for Uganda to assume the debt for the project if it is unsuccessful.

(   )   **4.**   The Americans suggested that Uganda and other Eastern African countries own 40% of the refinery.

(   )   **5.**   President Xi Jinping is eager to extend China's influence around the world.

Vocabulary

次の英文は、読売新聞の The Japan News「えいご工房」に掲載された *Can China dispel criticism of BRI as form of 'debt trap diplomacy'?*『一帯一路の「借金地獄外交」批判を拭えるか』の記事の一部です。下の語群から最も適切なものを１つ選び、(   ) 内に記入しなさい。

An international forum on the (   ) and Road Initiative, China's scheme to create a mega-economic zone, was held in Beijing, during which Chinese President Xi Jinping declared his nation would (   ) "high-quality" BRI projects.

Xi emphasized that when carrying out (   ) development, China will also abide by international rules.

China has probably attempted to modify its course of action in light of the adverse winds blowing (   ) the initiative.

There seems to be no end to voices (   ) out that many of those projects have disregarded the needs of target countries but prioritized the (   ) of Chinese companies. Criticism has also spread that the initiative has bound emerging countries to Beijing financially, by way of a "debt trap," so as to expand China's sphere of (   ).

It is a step forward that China's top official has indicated his idea of reviewing the initiative, but what is needed is action in (   ) with the words.

accordance	against	Belt	benefit
influence	infrastructure	pointing	pursue

- iPS 細胞での脊髄損傷治療計画実施承認
- iPS 細胞を用いたパーキンソン病治療の臨床試験

記者会見で iPS 細胞を使った脊髄損傷治療について説明する岡野慶応大学教授

Photo: Kyodo News

Before you read

下図は人体の各部位の名称です。空欄 1 〜 15 に入る適語を左記の語群から選びなさい。

a. abdomen
b. ankle
c. armpit
d. back
e. calf
f. elbow
g. forearm
h. knee
i. leg
j. neck
k. shoulder
l. thigh
m. toe
n. upperarm
o. wrist

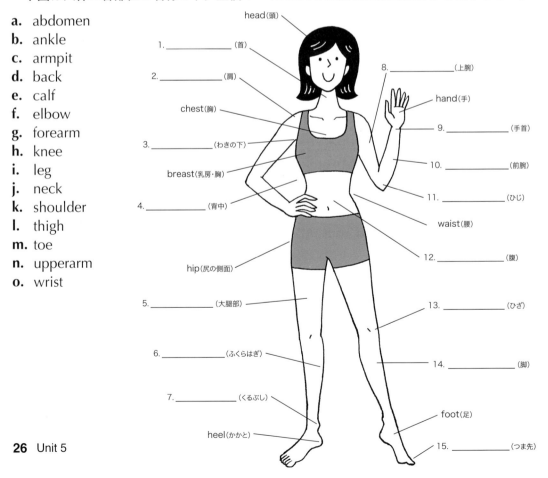

Words and Phrases

次の１～５の語句の説明として最も近いものをa～eから１つ選び、（　）内に記入しなさい。

1. authorize	（　　）	**a.**	officially recognize
2. undergo	（　　）	**b.**	confirm
3. neurological	（　　）	**c.**	likely to or in danger of
4. verify	（　　）	**d.**	receive or experience
5. prone to	（　　）	**e.**	related to the nerve system

Summary

次の英文は記事の要約です。下の語群から最も適切な語を１つ選び、（　　）内に記入しなさい。

Japanese scientists are making huge (　　　　　) in stem cell technology. Researchers at Keio will conduct (　　　　　) tests on people with spinal injuries. A Kyoto hospital has transplanted cells to (　　　　　) Parkinson's disease. Teams in Osaka are hoping to (　　　　　) cell (　　　　　) to help those with eye and heart diseases.

clinical　　perform　　strides　　transplants　　treat

令和時代は、科学がさらに発展し続け、iPS 細胞（人工多能性幹細胞）やゲノム編集などの最先端の生命科学は人の寿命を延ばし、AI（人工知能）は人の能力を拡張させるだろう。
狙った遺伝子を働かなくしたり、狙った場所に別の遺伝子を加えたりできる技術をゲノム編集と言われているが、効率的に遺伝子を改変できるようになった。病気の治療や農作物の品種改良などへの応用研究が進んでいる。また厚生労働省は、令和元年 6 月から患者から採取したがん細胞を分析し、遺伝子の変異を調べる「パネル検査」に公的な医療保険を適用することを決定した。がんに関連する遺伝子を解析し、効果的な治療薬を選ぶ「がんゲノム医療」が本格化する。
2006年に山中伸弥教授が開発した iPS 細胞は様々な細胞に変わり、無限に増殖する。目の難病加齢黄斑変性症の患者に iPS 細胞を注射して移植した。また、人の iPS 細胞から神経細胞を作って、パーキンソン病の患者の脳に移植した。この移植手術は、世界初となった。さらに脊髄損傷の患者に iPS 細胞を注入し移植する治療も進められている。iPS 細胞実用化に向けた動きが加速している。新たな生命科学技術に期待がかかる一方、より慎重な対応が求められる。

Reading

27

Spine injury iPS trial approved

World-first clinical test marks nation's
fifth authorized iPS study

The health ministry approved Monday the world's first
clinical test in which artificially derived stem cells will be
used to treat patients with spinal cord injuries.

A team of researchers from Keio University, which filed
5 a request for the test with the ministry, will inject neural cells
produced from so-called induced pluripotent stem cells —
known as iPS cells — into four people who sustained injuries
while playing sports or in traffic accidents.

28

The patients, aged 18 or older, will undergo the test
10 treatment under the care of a team led by Hideyuki Okano, a
professor at the School of Medicine.

The patients will have suffered lost mobility and sensation.
The cells will be injected within two to four weeks of the
patients' accidents — the period in which the treatment is
15 believed to be effective.

Every year some 5,000 people sustain spinal cord damage
in Japan, and the number of people living with some sort of
spinal cord-related injury is estimated to total over 100,000.

29

On Monday, a panel at the ministry also reviewed another
20 plan for a clinical test in which corneas produced from iPS
cells will be transplanted to treat eye diseases. The trial was
proposed by an Osaka University research team. The panel
did not reach a decision on the cornea trial, leaving further
consideration to future discussions.

25 Among other clinical tests with iPS cells, the government-
backed Riken institute conducted the world's first transplant
of retina cells grown from iPS cells to an individual with an
eye disease in 2014.

Kyoto University also began a clinical test using iPS cells
30 to treat Parkinson's disease last year.

The Japan times, Februrary 19, 2019

Spine injury：脊髄損傷
iPS：iPS 細胞《細胞を培養
　して人工的に作られた多
　能性の幹細胞；2006年に
　京都大学の山中伸弥教授
　らが世界で初めて作成に
　成功し、2012年にノーベ
　ル医学・生理学賞を受賞》
clinical test：臨床試験
authorized：公認の
health ministry：厚生労働省
artificially derived：人工由
　来の
stem cells：幹細胞
filed ～ with …：～を…に
　提出した
inject ～ into …：～を…
　に注入する
induced pluripotent stem
　cells：人工多能性多機能
　幹細胞

School of Medicine：医学部

lost mobility and
　sensation：運動機能や感
　覚機能を失ったこと

some sort of ～：何らかの
　～

panel：専門部会

corneas：（眼球の）角膜

further consideration：審理
　続行、継続

Riken institute：理化学研
　究所《埼玉県和光市に本
　部を置く自然科学系総合
　研究所；1917年設立》
retina：（眼球の）網膜

Parkinson's disease：パー
　キンソン病《脳の異常の
　ために体の動きに障害が
　現れる病気》

iPS cells used in treatment for Parkinson's

35　　Kyoto University said Friday it has conducted the world's first transplant of induced pluripotent stem cells to treat Parkinson's disease.

　　Parkinson's disease reduces dopamine-producing neurons in the brain and results in tremors in the hands and feet and
40　stiffness in the body. While there are treatments to relieve the symptoms, there is currently no cure for the disease. In Japan, an estimated 160,000 people suffer from the progressive neurological disorder and the number of patients is rising due to the graying of society.

45　　The clinical trial was carried out by the research center and Kyoto University Hospital, with doctors verifying the transplant's safety and effectiveness.

31

　　According to the treatment plan, the nerve cells transplanted into the patient's brain were created using iPS cells derived
50　from people who had types of immunity that made them less prone to rejecting transplants.

　　The study will involve seven patients in their 50s and 60s, who fulfilled the criteria of having received drug treatments without effective results and having suffered from Parkinson's
55　disease for more than five years.

　　Among other clinical trials related to regenerative medicine, Osaka University is planning to transplant heart muscle cell sheets derived from iPS cells into the hearts of patients who are suffering from serious heart failure.

The Japan Times, November 10, 2018

---

dopamine：ドーパミン《神経伝達物質の一種》

neurons：神経単位（細胞）

tremors：震え

stiffness：剛性、硬直

progressive neurological disorder：進行性の神経学的障害

graying：高齢化

research center：京都大学iPS細胞研究所

with doctors verifying ～：医師たちが～を確認しながら

immunity：免疫

less prone to ～：～しにくい

criteria：基準

regenerative medicine：再生医療

heart muscle cell sheets：心筋細胞シート

heart failure：心不全

Exercises

Multiple Choice

次の1〜5の英文を完成させるために、a〜dの中から最も適切なものを1つ選びなさい。

1. In Japan, the number of citizens who encounter some sort of spinal injury every year
   - **a.** is 5,000.
   - **b.** is all under 18.
   - **c.** exceeds 100,000.
   - **d.** reached 50,000.

2. Scientists believe that injections of iPS cells are most effective
   - **a.** at any time after the injury occurs.
   - **b.** within two to four weeks after the accident.
   - **c.** for patients having some sensation but lacking mobility.
   - **d.** for patients under the age of 18.

3. The types of iPS cell transplants being considered include
   - **a.** treatment for spinal cord injuries as an alternative to the usual medicines.
   - **b.** cornea and retina material produced from iPS cells.
   - **c.** heart muscle cell sheets to improve heart health.
   - **d.** all of the above applications of stem cell research.

4. The spinal surgery is believed
   - **a.** to be the first clinical test of iPS cells on patients suffering from backbone injuries.
   - **b.** to be able to help patients increase mobility and sensation.
   - **c.** to be the fifth authorized study of stem cells.
   - **d.** to show all of the above aspects of medical science.

5. The Parkinson iPS stem cell candidates
   - **a.** have had the disease for more than 5 years.
   - **b.** are 50-60 years of age.
   - **c.** hope to relieve symptoms of the disease like stiffness and tremors.
   - **d.** fulfill all of the above conditions.

本文の内容に合致するものに T（True）、合致しないものに F（False）をつけなさい。

(   )   **1.** The "graying of society" refers to a large segment of the population becoming older.

(   )   **2.** In Japan there are more than 100,000 people who suffer from a progressive neurological disorder.

(   )   **3.** Some types of heart failure might possibly be eliminated with the introduction of iPS stem cells into the heart muscle.

(   )   **4.** Physicians working at Kyoto University will attempt stem cell implantation in spinal cord injuries.

(   )   **5.** iPS stem cells are providing new hope for patients with formerly incurable afflictions.

Vocabulary

下図は、人体の各臓器と骨格の名称を記したものです。空欄(1)〜(15)に入る適語を右記の語群から選びなさい。

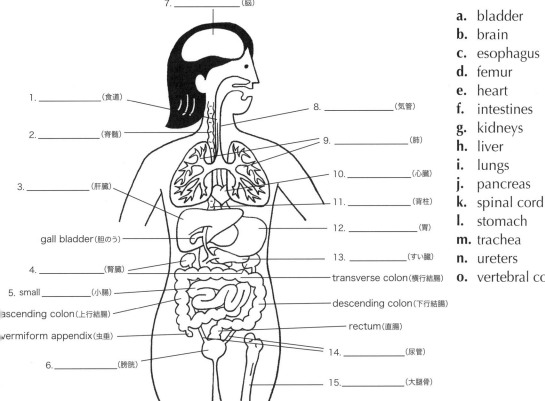

7. _____（脳）
1. _____（食道）
2. _____（脊髄）
3. _____（肝臓）
gall bladder（胆のう）
4. _____（腎臓）
5. small _____（小腸）
ascending colon（上行結腸）
vermiform appendix（虫垂）
6. _____（膀胱）
8. _____（気管）
9. _____（肺）
10. _____（心臓）
11. _____（背柱）
12. _____（胃）
13. _____（すい臓）
transverse colon（横行結腸）
descending colon（下行結腸）
rectum（直腸）
14. _____（尿管）
15. _____（大腿骨）

a. bladder
b. brain
c. esophagus
d. femur
e. heart
f. intestines
g. kidneys
h. liver
i. lungs
j. pancreas
k. spinal cord
l. stomach
m. trachea
n. ureters
o. vertebral column

●花崇拝を止めてコーランに

以前、森で暮らしていた花崇拝の心霊治療師が転居し、住む「モダーン」な家屋の壁飾り

Photo: The New York Times ／ Redux ／アフロ

Before you read

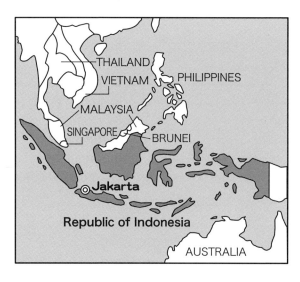

Republic of Indonesia
インドネシア共和国
オランダより1945年独立

面積　1,919,440km² （日本の約5倍）
人口　255,000,000人
公用語　インドネシア語
GDP　9,323億ドル
通貨　ルピア
首都　ジャカルタ
民族　大半がマレー人、他に300の民族
宗教　イスラム教　87.2%
　　　ヒンドゥ教　1.7% ／ 仏教　0.7%
　　　キリスト教　9.8%（プロテスタント6.9%）
　　　　　　　　　　　（カトリック2.9%）

識字率　88.5%
政体　共和制

Words and Phrases

次の1〜5の語句の説明として最も近いものをa〜eから1つ選び、(　)内に記入しなさい。

1. give way to　（　）　　　a. difficult to stop
2. offering　（　）　　　b. gift to a god or king or queen
3. rampant　（　）　　　c. get replaced by
4. fumes　（　）　　　d. leaves and greenery
5. foliage　（　）　　　e. smoke or gases

Summary

次の英文は記事の要約です。下の語群から最も適切な語を1つ選び、(　)内に記入しなさい。

32

Rubber and palm oil (　　　　) are destroying Indonesia's forests and the animals living there. Many forest (　　　　) have had to move to cities. Concrete buildings and artificial flowers are replacing their traditional (　　　　). Islam and Christianity are replacing their nature-(　　　　) religion. But to the government this is (　　　　).

centered　　dwellers　　environment　　production　　progress

インドネシアは、人口約2億6000万人、1万7000の島々からなる多民族国家で、中央と地方の格差が大きい。地方の電力や流通などのインフラ整備が遅れている。国民の約9割がイスラム教徒だが、イスラム教を国教と定めず、仏教徒やヒンドゥ教徒、キリスト教徒などに配慮を示して来た。しかし、近年イスラムの保守化が加速され、宗教間の摩擦が強まっている。

1000万人以上の人口が密集する首都ジャカルタの交通渋滞は深刻で、経済損失は年間100兆ルピア（約7,900億円）近くに上るとされる。2019年4月1日渋滞緩和策として、日本の企業がMRT大量高速鉄道を建設した。全長15.7キロメートルの区間を車だと2時間もかかることもあるのに、MRTは約30分で結ぶ。

2019年5月21日、ジョコ大統領が再選されたが、経済格差や宗教の違いによる分断が広がっており、山積する課題に直面している。また、交通渋滞、洪水被害も頻発している首都ジャカルタから移転する方針を決めた。

Reading

33

Flower worship gives way to the Quran

As a traditional healer of the Orang Rimba, or forest people, here on the Indonesian island of Sumatra, Temenggung Tarip had long depended on jungle blooms to conjure the divine for his seminomadic indigenous community. An offering of
5 colorful petals would bring the elephant god, skilled at curing toothaches, or the tiger god, helpful for those who had lost their way.

34

But timber, rubber, paper and palm oil plantations have encroached on the forests of Indonesia. Since 2000, about 15
10 percent of the nation's tree cover has disappeared. In Jambi, the central Sumatran province that is home to a few thousand Orang Rimba, the amount of deforestation is even higher, at 32 percent since the turn of the century, according to Global Forest Watch.

15 Over the past decade, most of the forest people of Jambi, Mr. Tarip included, have emerged from the jungle, driven both by the rampant deforestation and by an Indonesian government policy to settle these tribes of hunter-gatherers and farmers.

35

20 A court ruling five years ago was supposed to protect the right of indigenous peoples to live undisturbed in their native habitat, but corporate farming continued to encroach on the national park the Orang Rimba called home.

Now, only about 1,000 Orang Rimba families still live
25 in the rain forest. Particularly destructive to their way of life were the fires agro-industrialists set to clear the forests for plantations. Choking fumes drifted over Orang Rimba land. The wild animals that formed the backbone of their diet, along with wild yams, could not survive among the monoculture
30 plantations. Hunger stalked the Orang Rimba.

36

Since leaving the forest eight years ago, Mr. Tarip, who estimates that he is about 60, has converted to Islam, the

gives way to ～ : ～に取って代わられる	
traditional healer : 心霊治療家、呪術師	
Orang Rimba : 《クブ族；マレー人による蔑称でもあるため「森の民」と言われる》	
conjure ～ : ～を呪文で呼び出す	
petals : 花びら	
encroached on ～ : ～を侵害した	
tree cover : 木喰	
deforestation : 森林破壊	
Global Forest Watch : 《世界中の森林をほぼリアルタイムで監視するためのオープンソースの web アプリ》	
settle ～ : ～を定住させる	
native habitat : 生息環境	
destructive were the fires : 《倒置》	
destructive : 破壊をもたらす	
agro-industrialists : 農産業者《前述の corporate farming とほぼ同じ》	
formed the backbone of ～ : ～を支えている	
monoculture : 単作、単一栽培	
converted to ～ : ～に改宗した	

dominant religion of Indonesia. On national identity cards, a necessity for life outside the jungle, all Indonesians must

35 select from among six faiths. Animist flower worship is not among the choices.

Today, Mr. Tarip lives with his wife, Putri Tija Sanggul, in a concrete shell in Sarolangun, a three-day walk from the wilderness that used to be their home. The only reminder of

40 nature in their new house is a bunch of purple orchids that cascades down a wall. The flowers are plastic.

Missionaries, both Muslim and Christian, have tried to ease the transition to what the Orang Rimba call "the outside." Beyond the obvious differences — concrete walls, processed

45 food, brightly colored plastic — the outside is confounding in other ways. The forest was cool, sunlight barely penetrating the dense foliage. Concrete, by contrast, holds the heat. Sleeping in the stuffy confines of his home is something to which Mr. Tarip is still not accustomed.

50 As a community leader, one who lives in a proper concrete house with plastic flowers, Mr. Tarip was hailed by a former governor of Jambi as a role model for the Orang Rimba. He has ridden in an elevator and in an airplane, which took him to Mecca for an all-expenses-paid pilgrimage.

The New York Times International Edition, October 16, 2018

---

faiths：信仰
Animist：精霊信仰の

cascades down 〜：〜を滝のように垂れ下がる
Missionaries：伝道者

confusing：人を当惑させる

penetrating 〜：〜を通して差し込む
foliage：枝葉

in the stuffy confines of his home：風通しの悪い部屋に閉じこめられて

hailed as 〜：〜としてもてはやされた
role model for 〜：〜の手本となる人物

Mecca：メッカ《サウジアラビアにあるイスラム教最大の聖地であり、祈りを捧げる対象》
all-expenses-paid：全て経費が無料で
pilgrimage：巡礼

Exercises

次の1の英文の質問に答え、2〜5の英文を完成させるために、a〜dの中から最も適切なものを1つ選びなさい。

1. What is happening in the rain forests of Indonesia?

    a. Plantations for timber, palm oil, and paper creation are causing the forest to disappear.

    b. Mr. Tarip has forced the Orang Rimba people to continue to be semi-nomadic.

    c. A blight has taken over the forest, causing the trees to die or be chopped down.

    d. The Indonesian government is trying to limit the number of plantations.

2. The original religion of most Orang Rimba people was

    a. based on ancestors.   **c.** centered around flowers.

    b. Islam.   **d.** Christianity.

3. Orang Rimba people believe that offering flower petals to the elephant god will

    a. get rid of a headache.   **c.** reward you with food.

    b. assist you if you become lost. **d.** get rid of your toothache.

4. Mr. Tarip lives in a concrete house and finds

    a. it quite hot because there are no trees around to give shade.

    b. different and distant from where he used to live.

    c. only plastic flowers nearby, making him miss the forest.

    d. all of the above things difficult to get used to.

5. Since the turn of the century, the deforestation of trees in Jambi has risen to

    a. 15%.   **c.** 10%.

    b. 32%.   **d.** 38%.

本文の内容に合致するものに T（True）、合致しないものに F（False）をつけなさい。

(   ) **1.** The Orang Rimba have to deal with hunger because the animals and wild yams that they used to eat are dying from too many monoculture plantations burning the forest to build plantations.

(   ) **2.** The Orang Rimba were not happy to be hunters and farmers.

(   ) **3.** The Orang Rimba can be described as "forest people" of Sumatra.

(   ) **4.** Mr. Tarip has traveled to Mecca on an all-expense paid pilgrimage.

(   ) **5.** The legal system recognizes the Orang Rimba people's right to live in the forest, but authorities have not supported it.

Vocabulary

次の英文は、The New York Times International Edition に掲載された *How religion dominates Indonesia's politics*『いかに宗教がインドネシア政治を独占しているか』の記事の一部です。下の語群から最も適切なものを1つ選び、（   ）内に記入しなさい。

Mr. Joko Widodo and Mr. Prabowo Subianto are scheduled to meet for their second debate on Feb. 17, and the agenda will focus on natural resources, (   ) and the environment. But soon enough, the main issue of this election – (   )– will return to the fore.

In the last four years, Mr. Joko has offered a modicum of hope to (   ) and pro-democratic groups. He is not an ideal figure and has been (   ) in dealing with human rights issues like military violence against civilians. But there is no other (   ).

Regional ordinances to accommodate Shariah law have multiplied, the result of the relative autonomy of some regions. The specifics (   ), ranging from the call for city officials to wear Muslim (   ) to the ban on the sale, distribution and (   ) of alcohol. More absurd and more frightening are the movements for underage marriage and against vaccines.

choice	consumption	dress	infrastructure
progressive	religion	slow	vary

Unit 7

● ベネズエラから徒歩で脱出

アンデス山中を徒歩で「移動」するベネズエラ難民たち

Photo: The New York Times ／ Redux ／アフロ

Before you read

**Bolivarian Republic of Venezuela
ベネズエラ・ボリバル共和国**

面積　912,050km² （日本の約2.4倍）
人口　31,020,000人
首都　カラカス
公用語　スペイン語
民族　混血　67%　／ ヨーロッパ系　21%
　　　アフリカ系　10%　／ インド系　2%
宗教　キリスト教・カトリック　92%
　　　　　　　　　プロテスタント　6%
　　　ユダヤ教　1.1%　／ イスラム教　0.9%
GDP　3,807億ドル
通貨　ボリバル・フエルテ　→　ソベラノ
識字率　95.5%
政体　共和制

次の１〜５の語句の説明として最も近いものをa〜eから１つ選び、（　　）内に記入しなさい。

1. lot	（　）		**a.**	demonstrate or reveal
2. crackdown	（　）		**b.**	strong reaction against protest
3. pass	（　）		**c.**	space or area
4. speak to	（　）		**d.**	way of surviving economically
5. livelihood	（　）		**e.**	high valley

Summary

次の英文は記事の要約です。下の語群から最も適切な語を１つ選び、（　　）内に記入しなさい。

38

　　The (　　　　　　) economic situation in Venezuela has (　　　　　　) a political crisis. People are (　　　　　　) not only from power and food shortages but also from violence, as challenges to President Maduro (　　　　　　). More than three million have left so far, with many (　　　　　　) a long, cold and dangerous journey on foot over the mountains into Colombia.

fleeing　　mount　　perilous　　risking　　triggered

　　2013年３月チャベス大統領死去後、４月には後継指名を受けたマドゥロ氏が大統領選で当選した。翌2014年には、世界最大級の原油埋蔵量を誇るベネズエラに原油価格下落で外貨不足に陥り、政策の失敗もあって財政が悪化し、経済は破綻状態に追い込まれた。

　　激しい物価上昇が続く中、2018年５月にマドゥロ氏が再選されたが、トランプ米政権はベネズエラに経済制裁を決定した。同年８月に通貨の単位を10万分の１に切り下げるデノミネーションを実施した。通貨単位「ボリバル・フェルテ」からゼロを５つ減らした新しい単位「ボリバル・ソベラノ」を導入した。インフレ率は約170万％で国民生活は限界に近づき、食料等の生活必需品や医薬品が不足し、停電が続き、治安の悪化や生活苦で、人口の１割に当たる約330万人が隣国コロンビアやブラジルなどに逃れたとされる。

　　2019年１月10日反米左派のマドゥロ大統領が２期目をスタートさせた。中国やロシアと関係強化を図り、イラン、トルコ、キューバ、メキシコ、ボリビアからも支持されている。一方、野党指導者のグアイド国会議長が暫定大統領就任を宣言した。米国、ブラジル、コロンビア、アルゼンチン、チリ、ペルー、カナダ、英独仏など19か国がグアイド氏を承認した。２月下旬に国境閉鎖し、人道支援物資搬入を阻止していたが、６月８日にはタチラ州のコロンビアとの国境封鎖を解除した。

Reading

39

Fleeing Venezuela, on foot

Their lives shattered, millions try to escape the country's economic crisis

The walking began before dawn: before the clouds broke against the mountaintops, before the trucks took over the highway, even before anyone in the town woke up to check the vacant lot where scores of Venezuelan refugees had been 5 huddling through the night.

Children, grandmothers, teachers, nurses, oil workers and the jobless had all sprawled there together — bound by a collective will to put as many miles as possible between themselves and the collapsing country they had fled.

40

10 All but Yoxalida Pimentel. She could not take another step.

"After so many hours of walking, after days, nights, sun, cold, rain — I lost my baby," she said, crying alone the morning after her miscarriage.

15 The economic crisis that has engulfed Venezuela under President Nicolás Maduro has set off a staggering exodus. The economic damage is among the worst in Latin American history, researchers say, with more than three million people leaving the country in recent years — largely on foot.

41

20 They are fleeing dangerous shortages of food, water, electricity and medicine, as well as the government's political crackdowns, in which more than 40 people have been killed in the last few weeks alone.

Rolling suitcases behind them, some walk along highways, 25 their salaries so obliterated by Venezuela's hyperinflation that bus tickets are out of reach. Others try to hitchhike the thousands of miles to reach Ecuador or Peru.

But no matter their destination, the vast majority come through treacherous roads in Colombia: a 125-mile journey 30 that includes a 12,000-foot pass in the Andes Mountains.

Fleeing 〜：〜から逃げる	
shattered：砕け散った	
vacant lot：空き地	
refugees：避難民	
huddling：身を寄せ合う	
sprawled：寝そべっていた	
collective will：全体の意思	
collapsing：崩壊しつつある	
All but 〜：〜を除いては	
miscarriage：流産	
engulfed 〜：〜を巻き込んだ	
staggering exodus：（人を）非常に驚かせるほどの脱出	
medicine：医薬品	
crackdowns：弾圧	
obliterated：消失した	
destination：目的地	
pass：峠、山道	

42

"It's the coldest place I've known in my life," said Fredy Rondón, who had come from Venezuela's capital, Caracas, with a single bag of belongings. Now, he was breathless at 10,500 feet, with a treeless steppe before him.

35 "I thought I could take the cold, but this is too, too much," he said.

His willingness to travel the twisting mountain roads speaks to the desperation in Venezuela. The country is experiencing its deepest political unrest in a generation, with 40 two men claiming the presidency simultaneously.

43

Here in the Colombian mountains, Venezuelan refugees murmur about Juan Guaidó, the opposition leader who declared himself Venezuela's legitimate leader last month, inspiring many Venezuelans to rally to his side. The opposition and Mr. 45 Maduro are at loggerheads over the delivery of humanitarian aid that Mr. Maduro's government has blockaded at the border with Colombia.

"We are all scared it will get ugly between Maduro and Guaidó," said Norma López, who walked with her five 50 children and 6-day-old infant.

The road seemed endless. But not far from the summit, a miracle happened: A giant, empty truck pulled over.

"When you have no load, you have to take them," said the driver, who asked not to be named. "But the truth is you risk 55 your livelihood too if the company finds out or the police stop you."

The New York Times International Edition, February 22, 2019

speaks to 〜：〜を証明する
desperation：絶望
unrest：不安
claiming 〜：〜は自分の物 だと主張する

opposition：野党

legitimate：合法的
inspire 〜 to …：〜に…さ せる

at loggerheads over 〜： 〜を巡って喧嘩している
humanitarian aid：人道援助

scared 〜：〜を恐れている
get ugly：険悪なムードに なる

pulled over：停まった

asked not to be named： 匿名を希望した

Exercises

Multiple Choice

次の１〜５の英文を完成させるために、ａ〜ｄの中から最も適切なものを１つ選びなさい。

1. The people of Venezuela

   a. are happy to be living in such a peaceful country.

   b. have no desire to go to Peru or Ecuador.

   c. are fleeing their country and President Maduro.

   d. can survive because of the economic policies of the new president.

2. The "leaving the country" process is dangerous because of

   a. the mountain roads and passes crossing the Andes.

   b. having to endure their long journey on foot.

   c. the risk of getting caught in political crackdowns.

   d. all of the problems involved in the exodus.

3. More people do not take the bus on their trip because

   a. the inflation in the country has made the price of a bus ticket too expensive.

   b. there is no bus service towards Ecuador or Peru.

   c. going on foot is more exciting as they are with relatives and friends.

   d. buses are undependable, especially on winding mountain roads.

4. People are fleeing Venezuela because of

   a. a lack of medicine.　　**c.** a lack of water and electricity.

   b. a lack of food.　　**d.** all of the above hardships.

5. President Maduro and opposition leader Juan Guaidó disagree about

   a. Latin American history.

   b. allowing humanitarian supplies into the country.

   c. diplomatic policy toward Peru.

   d. giving rides to people traveling on foot.

True or False

本文の内容に合致するものに T（True）、合致しないものに F（False）をつけなさい。

( ) **1.** Citizens hope that activity between Maduro and Guaidó will not become violent.

( ) **2.** President Maduro takes full responsibility for the inflation and shortage of food and necessities for the Venezuelans.

( ) **3.** The Andes Mountains pass exposed fleeing citizens from Venezuela to freezing weather conditions.

( ) **4.** This article might assume that Juan Guaidó would be the preferred head of Venezuela by its citizens.

( ) **5.** Mr. Maduro has agreed to open the blockade at the Colombian border.

Vocabulary

次のクロスワードパズルを、下の Across 横、Down 縦の英文説明を読んで、Unit 12 の記事から最も適切な語を見つけ、□の中に 1 文字ずつ入れないさい。。

ACROSS
- 1 run away
- 4 happening at the same
- 5 top of a mountain
- 6 leader of Venezuela
- 8 thousand thousands
- 9 an amazing and lucky event

DOWN
- 2 country in South America
- 3 frightened and without hope
- 4 lack
- 7 sunrise

●国境での米国の恥

ホンジュラスから歩いて米国を目指す人たち

Photo: AP／アフロ

Before you read

United States of America
アメリカ合衆国

面積　9,628,000km² （世界３位・日本の約25.4倍）
人口　316,942,000人 （世界３位）
首都　ワシントンDC　/ **最大都市　ニューヨーク**
公用語　なし、事実上は英語　/ **識字率** 93.5%
人種　白人 72.4%　/ ヒスパニック 18.5%
　　　黒人 12.6%　/ アジア系 4.8%
　　　ネイティブアメリカン 0.9%
宗教　キリスト教・カトリック 21%
　　　　　　　　　プロテスタント 58%
　　　ユダヤ教 1.3%　/ イスラム教 0.9%
　　　無宗教 22.8%
GDP　18兆5691億ドル （世界１位）
通貨　US ドル

United Mexican States
メキシコ合衆国

面積　1,972,550km² （日本の約５倍）
人口　129,200,000人　/ 首都　メキシコシティ
公用語　スペイン語　/ 識字率 99%
人種　混血 60%　/ 先住民 30%
　　　ヨーロッパ系 9%　/ その他 1%
宗教　キリスト教・カトリック 90%
GDP　１兆2609億ドル　/ **通貨** メキシコペソ

次の１〜５の語の説明として最も近いものを a〜e から１つ選び、(　　)内に記入しなさい。

1. disgrace　　　　(　　)　　**a.** preference
2. rally　　　　　 (　　)　　**b.** terribly sad
3. posture　　　　 (　　)　　**c.** shame
4. harrowing　　　 (　　)　　**d.** encourage
5. priority　　　　 (　　)　　**e.** position or opinion

Summary

次の英文は記事の要約です。下の語群から最も適切な語を１つ選び、(　　)内に記入しなさい。

44

Trump's (　　　　　　) attitude to refugees is well known. However, the border crisis is such an emotional topic that his opponents are also (　　　　　) to offer practical solutions. While the (　　　　　) of words between Republicans and Democrats continues, thousands (　　　　　). Economic migrants may have to wait so that those escaping violence can be given (　　　　　).

battle　　failing　　priority　　suffer　　unsympathetic

1994年に Operation Gatekeeper by California, Operation Safeguard by Arizona, Operation Hold-the-Line by Texas の３大作戦の一環として、Bill Clinton 大統領の下で、「Mexico − United States barrier メキシコとアメリカの壁」が建設された。メキシコからアメリカ合衆国への中南米で作られた麻薬の密輸、不法移民の密入国を防ぐことを目的としたアメリカとメキシコ国境に沿った一連の壁とフェンスである。アメリカとメキシコの国境は、3,145km あり、４州の都市部や砂漠、山地を横切っている。930km 以上のフェンスが建設されているが、一続きの壁ではなく、単距離のものである。壁が設置されていない区間は、センサーと監視カメラによる「仮想フェンス」が敷かれ、国境警備隊によってモニタリングされている。

Trump 大統領は、2016年の選挙中に国境の壁建設を公約した。2019年には国境警備関連予算70億ドル（約7600億円）を議会に求めたが、承認を得られなかった。メキシコからの不法移民は減少しているが、中米グアテマラ、ホンジュラス、エルサルバトルからの不法移民が貧困から逃れてやってきている。

Reading

Our Disgrace At the Border

SUPPOSE ONE NIGHT there is a knock on your door. You open it to find 100 bedraggled families shivering in your yard — exhausted, filthy, terrified. The first cry of your heart would be to take them in, but you'd know there were too many.

5　But you'd still do something. You'd rally your neighbors and the local authorities and put some system in place — some way to provide immediate care, figure out who these people were and how, within your means, you could lift them up.

10　And this is precisely what the U.S. has failed to do in handling the refugees who are flooding across the southern border. There is nothing remotely like an adequate system in place to handle the hundreds of thousands of people fleeing violence in Central America or seeking economic opportunity. 15 And there is no prospect of a plan being put in place from either Republicans or Democrats.

And in that way the border crisis is paradigmatic of our politics right now. Both parties are content to adopt abstract ideological postures. Neither is interested in creating a 20 functioning system that balances trade-offs and actually works. In the age of Trump, national politics is showbiz — self-righteous performance art to make the base feel good about itself.

The Trump show is all about toughness and cruelty. The 25 administration adopted a zero-tolerance policy that was supposed to deter potential immigrants. It failed miserably. Roughly 103,000 unauthorized immigrants reached the U.S.-Mexico border in March, twice as many as in March 2018.

Aside from baring his fangs, Trump is uninterested in 30 processing the extra refugees.

The field is wide open for the Democrats to come forth with a decent plan. But on many issues the 2020 Democrats

SUPPOSE ～：仮に～だと思う
bedraggled：雨で衣服が濡れた、みすぼらしい

rally ～：～を呼び集める
put ～ in place：～を配備する
figure out ～：～だと分かる
within your means：あなたの出来る範囲以内で

nothing like ～：～とは別物である
in place：機能している

put in place：導入される
Republicans：共和党
Democrats：民主党
paradigmatic of ～：～と連合関係にある、連動している
trade-offs：妥協、取り決め

self-righteous：自己中心的な
base feel good about itself：自分がよい気持ちになる《make は使役》
zero-tolerance：いかなる違反も許さない、断固とした
deter ～：～を阻止する

Aside from ～：～を除いて
baring his fangs：牙を剥(む)く

aren't really having a primary campaign; they're having a purity test. So the Democratic show consists of indignant generalities intended to sound radical while changing nothing.

Many Democrats in Congress are denying there even is a crisis on the border. The only Democratic candidate with an immigration plan so far is Julián Castro, who wants to repeal a 1929 provision that made illegal entry a federal crime.

Immigration is one of those issues on which the extreme positions are wrong, because the correct answer means balancing competing goods.

On the one hand, these people are our neighbors. Many of them come to us with harrowing stories of husbands murdered, daughters raped, mass extortion.

On the other hand, many who are coming across seeking asylum do not qualify for it. When they get their hearings, only 20 percent win the right to stay in the United States because they'd face persecution in their home countries. Many come for traditional economic reasons.

The U.S. cannot take in everybody who wants to come. So the first task is to set priorities. The victims of violence and persecution get top priority, then those being systemically denied their basic rights because their country has become a failed state, then those seeking economic betterment.

by David Brooks

The New York Times, April 12, 2019

purity test：純度試験《基礎票のみで浮動票なし》
generalities：一般論
Congress：米連邦議会
repeal ～：～を廃止する
provision：規定
competing goods：競合品
harrowing：悲惨な、痛ましい
extortion：強奪
asylum：保護施設、避難所
get their hearings：審理を受ける
persecution：迫害
set priorities：優先順位を付ける
failed state：失敗（破綻・機能不全）国家

Exercises

Multiple Choice

次の1〜3の質問に答え、4〜5の英文を完成させるために、a〜dの中から最も適切なものを1つ選びなさい。

1. Which does the author think is the strongest reason for getting asylum in the U.S.?

    a. Ability to create a better economic future for one's family in the U.S.

    b. Denying other people's basic human rights.

    c. Being a victim of violence and persecution in one's home country.

    d. Ability to easily assimilate into the U.S.

2. What percentage of refugees qualify for asylum on the basis of facing violence at home?

    a. 10%   **c.** 30%

    b. 20%   **d.** 12%

3. How does the U.S. plan to handle the thousands of citizens who wish to come in?

    a. Mr. Trump has a plan that is cruel and tough towards refugees.

    b. The Democrats have generalized ideas, but have not taken steps to form them into a plan.

    c. The Republicans have devised few detailed plans beyond showing support for Mr. Trump's ideas.

    d. All of the above describe the current situation regarding refugee planning.

4. Some Democrats

    a. are very concerned about Mr. Trump's self-righteousness but offer very few real solutions.

    b. have come up with several specific plans to help the refugees.

    c. agree with the government on separating parents from children.

    d. have promised to provide schooling for the children.

5. The author relates a story about Americans

    a. helping others who have come to them for assistance.

    b. seeking asylum in other countries.

    c. turning away those in trouble from their neighborhood.

    d. committing rape and murder against refugees.

本文の内容に合致するものに T（True）、合致しないものに F（False）をつけなさい。

(   ) **1.** Mr. Trump appears to be a man who considers only himself and his family.

(   ) **2.** Congress in the U.S. is supposed to represent its citizens, but has shown little action to date.

(   ) **3.** Three times as many immigrants reached the U.S./Mexico border this year than in past years.

(   ) **4.** Julián Castro wants to repeal the law that made illegal entry into the U.S. a federal crime.

(   ) **5.** An immigrant seeking a better economic situation might not be allowed to work in the U.S.

Vocabulary

次の英文は、The New York Times International Edition に掲載された *Border desperation grows. So do smugglers' fees.* 『国境でのパニックはつのり、密入国業者の費用も上がるばかりだ』の記事の一部です。下の語群から最も適切なものを 1 つ選び、(   ) 内に記入しなさい。

The Trump administration, which has partially shut down the federal government in a fight over (   ) for an enhanced border (   ), has adopted a number of strategies over the last two years to deter (   ) and persuade them to turn around – or not to come at all.

Its latest effort is a policy that admits only a few (   ) seekers a day, if that, at border crossings. As a result of this metering, migrants are now waiting on the Mexican side of the border for weeks and months before they can submit their (   ).

In Reynosa, Mexico and elsewhere, the delays caused by the policy are prompting many migrants to (   ) the costs and dangers of a faster option: hiring a (   ), at an increasingly high rate, to sneak them into the United States. The number of migrant families caught attempting to cross the border skyrocketed to its (   ) levels on record.

applications	asylum	funding	highest
migrants	smuggler	wall	weigh

Unit 9

●大統領にユダヤ人が選ばれ、心穏やかでないウクライナのユダヤ人

ウクライナ大統領選挙で勝利宣言するユダヤ系のゼレンスキー氏　　Photo: ロイター／アフロ

Before you read

Ukraine　ウクライナ
1991年8月ソビエト連邦より独立

面積　603,700km^2（日本の約1.6倍）
人口　42,410,000人（クリミアを除く）
首都　キエフ
公用語　ウクライナ語
民族　ウクライナ人　77.8%
　　　ロシア人　17.3%　／ベラルーシ人　0.6%
　　　モルドバ、クリミア・タタール人、
　　　ユダヤ人
宗教　ウクライナ正教会　76.5%
　　　ユダヤ教　0.6%
　　　ウクライナ東方カトリック教会　14.7%
　　　ローマカトリック　2.2%
　　　プロテスタント　2.2%
GDP　1,093億ドル　／ **通貨**　フリヴニア
識字率　99.7%
政体　共和制

次の１〜５の語の説明として最も近いものをa〜eから１つ選び、（　　）内に記入しなさい。

1. recall　　　　　　（　　）　　**a.** successfully deal with
2. scarred　　　　　（　　）　　**b.** by a large margin
3. wildly　　　　　　（　　）　　**c.** violent and tragic
4. overcome　　　　（　　）　　**d.** remember
5. congregation　　（　　）　　**e.** group united by a common belief

Summary

次の英文は記事の要約です。下の語群から最も適切な語を１つ選び、（　　）内に記入しなさい。

50

（　　　　　　　　） Ukraine has a history of discrimination against Jews, it mostly occurred (　　　　　　) the country became independent. (　　　　　　) there is little anti-Semitism, yet some Jewish Ukrainians worry that the election of a Jewish president will lead to (　　　　　) hostility against them. A rabbi from Dnipro feels these people should stop (　　　　　) in the past.

although　　before　　living　　nowadays　　renewed

2019年４月、コメディ俳優ゼレンスキー氏がウクライナの新大統領に就任した。政治の素人という清新さが支持を集めて圧勝したが、議会に支持勢力を持たず、政権運営の懸念材料となっている。就任演説で「クリミアと東部地域はウクライナの大地」と強調し、さらにロシアとの対話の用意があると述べた。ヨーロッパとロシアの間に位置するウクライナの混乱はヨーロッパ全体の安全保障に悪影響を及ぼすため、ゼレンスキー新大統領の対ロシア政策が問われている。

ウクライナ国土のほとんどが平坦な丘陵地で、南部ステップ地帯には肥沃な黒土が広がる。ウクライナの行政単位は、24の州とクリミア半島にあるクリミア自治共和国、そして２つの特別市から構成されている。クリミア自治共和国は、クリミア半島のうち、ウクライナの特別市セヴァストポリを除いた地域を管轄していた。2014年のクリミア危機においてロシアと親ロシア派の自警団がクリミア自治共和国を掌握して、住民投票を実施した。結果、「クリミア共和国」として、セヴァストポリ市と共にロシア連邦に編入された。

1894年にウクライナ生まれのユダヤ人作家ショーレム・アレイヘムは短編小説『牛乳屋テヴィ』を書き、後にその作品が「屋根の上のバイオリン弾き」として上演された。帝政ロシア領ウクライナに暮らすユダヤ教徒の生活を描いたものだが、ユダヤ人に対するPogrom 集団的迫害排斥が行われていた。

51

Some Ukraine Jews Are Unhappy a Jew Was Elected President

DNIPRO, Ukraine — When Volodymyr Zelensky, the Jewish comedian recently elected the president of Ukraine, announced that he was running, the chief rabbi for the eastern Ukrainian region where Mr. Zelensky grew up was shocked
5 by the hostile reaction.

But the opposition, Rabbi Shmuel Kaminezki said, did not come from the Orthodox Church, a bastion of anti-Semitism in the past, or from a Ukrainian nationalist movement that collaborated with the Nazis during Hitler's invasion of the
10 Soviet Union. They could not seem to care less that Mr. Zelensky was a Jew, the rabbi recalled.

Instead, the hostility came from Mr. Zelensky's fellow Jews, both secular and religious, for whom painful memories of czarist-era pogroms and the Holocaust are still very much
15 alive.

"They said, 'He should not run because we will have pogroms here again in two years if things go wrong,'" said Rabbi Kaminezki, the chief rabbi in Dnipro, the capital of Ukraine's Dnipropetrovsk region.

20 Despite its scarred history, Ukraine today is no hotbed of anti-Semitism. It already has a Jewish prime minister, Volodymyr Groysman, and if he stays on after Mr. Zelensky is sworn in, Ukraine will be the only country outside of Israel where the heads of state and government are Jewish.

25 Religion barely came up during the campaign.

The reason, said Igor Shchupak, a Holocaust historian in Dnipro, is that past persecution of Jews was carried out mostly when Ukraine's territory was under the control of foreign states, principally Russia and Germany, that made
30 anti-Semitism official policy.

"We have anti-Semites today, but we have no anti-

Jews：ユダヤ人《ユダヤ教信者を指す》

DNIPRO：ドニプロ《ウクライナ東部のドニプロペトローワシク州にある都市》

running：立候補する

chief rabbi：ユダヤ教の宗教的指導者、ラビ（師）

Orthodox Church：ウクライナ正教会《キリスト教の中の東方正教会の一つ》

anti-Semitism：反ユダヤ主義

nationalist movement：民族主義的運動

collaborated with ～：～に協力した

invasion：侵攻

not care less ～：～を何とも思っていない

secular：宗教的でない

czarist-era pogroms：ロシア帝政時代の大虐殺

Holocaust：ホロコースト《ナチスによるユダヤ人の大虐殺》

scarred：傷だらけの

stays on：留任する

heads of state and government：国家と政府のトップ（大統領と首相）

Semitism as a state policy," he said.

54

A survey by the Pew Research Center found that only 5 percent of Ukrainians surveyed would not accept Jews as
35 fellow citizens, compared with 18 percent of Poles, 22 percent of Romanians and 23 percent of Lithuanians. Ukraine now has the world's third- or fourth-largest Jewish community, but estimates of its size vary wildly, ranging from 120,000 to 400,000 people, depending on who is counting.

40 "The times of pogroms are over," Rabbi Kaminezki said. "This is not on anybody's agenda here."

Nevertheless, Rabbi Kaminezki said a big part of his job was getting local Jews to overcome what he called their "very high anxiety level" in a community still traumatized by
45 pogroms and the Holocaust. "The Jews left Egypt, but Egypt has not left the Jews," he said.

55

Rabbi Kaminezki said he had told his fretful congregation in Dnipro's main synagogue that they should welcome, not reject, a Jew running for the presidency.

50 The rabbi, a member of the Chabad movement that has spearheaded efforts to revive Jewish faith across the former Soviet Union, said he had advised Dnipro's Jews to shed what he called the "oy-vey complex" —— the tendency to fear the worst and shy away from their Jewishness.

55 "If you are not proud of yourself and your community, you will be not be accepted," he said he told them.

The New York Times, April 25, 2019

Pew Research Center：ピュー研究所《ワシントンにある、人々の問題意識や意見、傾向に関する情報を調査するシンクタンク；2004年設立》
fellow citizens：同胞

on agenda：議題に予定されている

getting local Jews to overcome：《使役》
anxiety level：不安レベル
traumatized：心に傷を負った
The Jews left Egypt：《キリスト教の旧約聖書中の「出エジプト記」を指す》
Egypt has not left the Jews：エジプトでの記憶はユダヤ人の心から決して離れることはない
congregation：信徒たち
Chabad movement：ハバド・ルバヴィッチ派運動《神秘主義のメシア待望論者の運動で、パレスチナにユダヤ民族の故郷を再建しようする》
spearheaded 〜：〜を陣頭指揮した
shed 〜：〜を棄てる
oy-vey：あらまあ、やれやれ《うろたえ、諦め、驚きなどを表すイディッシュ語［中・東欧のユダヤ人の間で話されていたドイツ語に近い言葉]》
shy away from 〜：〜を避ける

Exercises

次の１～５の英文を完成させるために、ａ～ｄの中から最も適切なものを１つ選びなさい。

1. According to Rabbi Kaminezki, recent opposition to Zelensky

   a. is because of his support of Soviet and German policies.

   b. has come from Ukrainian Jews themselves.

   c. is something to be welcomed.

   d. has nothing to do with the country's history.

2. Some of Ukraine's Jews fear a Jewish president will bring

   a. an invasion by Russia.   c. pogroms.

   b. 18% more Polish citizens.   d. greater respect for their religion.

3. When Zelensky announced for president, most citizens

   a. laughed because he was known as a comedian.

   b. had little interest in discussing religion.

   c. thought the country had become a hotbed of anti-Semitism.

   d. started making plans to move to Israel.

4. The population of Jews in the Ukraine

   a. has stayed more or less the same over the years.

   b. could be anything from 120,000 to 400,00 people.

   c. discourages Poles and Lithuanians from becoming citizens.

   d. encourages Jewish immigration into the Ukraine.

5. The Holocaust

   a. took place during the Czarist era.

   b. is not something Ukrainian Jews think about any more.

   c. explains how Zelensky was able to be elected president.

   d. still arouses fear and pain in Jewish people.

本文の内容に合致するものに T（True）、合致しないものに F（False）をつけなさい。

(   ) **1.** The Ukraine already seems to accept Jews in the government.

(   ) **2.** Pogroms and the Holocaust memories are just distant memories for Jews today.

(   ) **3.** Anti-semitism exists as a state policy in the Ukraine.

(   ) **4.** The highest percentage of hostility toward a Jewish president came from Lithuanians at 23%.

(   ) **5.** The Ukraine is going to be one of two countries whose heads of state and government are both Jewish.

Vocabulary

次の 1〜8 は、旧ソ連の国々に関する英文です。下記の国名から 1 つ選び（   ）内に、a〜h を地図から選び、[   ] 内に記入しなさい。

1. (   ) is bordered on the west by the Black Sea and its capital is Tbilisi.   [   ]

2. (   ) is on the east coast of the Baltic Sea and its capital is Vilnius.   [   ]

3. (   ) has borders with Poland, Latvia, Lithuania, Russia, and Ukraine.   [   ]

4. (   ) 's capital is Kiev.   [   ]

5. (   ) is next to the Caspian Sea and its capital is Baku.   [   ]

6. (   ) is bordered on the west by Romania and on the east by Ukraine.   [   ]

7. (   ) 's capital is Tallinn.   [   ]

8. (   ) has borders with Turkey, Iran, Georgia, and Azerbaijan. [   ]

Armenia	Azerbaijan
Belarus	Estonia
Georgia	Lithuania
Moldova	Ukraine

●イラン革命40周年でイデオロギーによる日常生活の支配が緩む

イランのテヘラン市内での通勤バス風景　　Photo: The New York Times ／ Redux ／アフロ

Before you read

Islamic Republic of Iran
イラン・イスラム共和国
1979年4月1日イラン・イスラム革命後共和国が樹立された

面積　1,648,195km^2（日本の約4.4倍）
人口　80,000,000人
首都　テヘラン
公用語　ペルシャ語
民族　ペルシャ人　61%　／クルド人　10%
　　　アゼルバイジャン人　35%
　　　ロル族　6%
宗教　イスラム教・シーア派　90%
　　　　　　　　スンニ派　9%
　　　キリスト教・ゾロアスター教・ユダヤ
　　　教等　1%
GDP　4,319億ドル　／ **通貨**　イラン・リヤル
識字率　85%
政治　イスラム共和制

次の1～5の語の説明として最も近いものをa～eから1つ選び、(　　)内に記入しなさい。

1. ideology　　　(　　)　　**a.** according to the rules
2. rickety　　　 (　　)　　**b.** enthusiastic support
3. amputation　 (　　)　　**c.** cutting off a limb
4. fervor　　　 (　　)　　**d.** belief system
5. technically　 (　　)　　**e.** weak

Summary

次の英文は記事の要約です。下の語群から最も適切な語を1つ選び、(　　)内に記入しなさい。

56

　Forty years ago a (　　　　　　) gave Iranians hope for a better society. But the politics of a western-leaning autocrat was replaced by the politics of (　　　　) Islam. In public, people had to obey strict rules about clothing and (　　　　　). At home, however, they led more (　　　　) lives. (　　　　), life has been getting more relaxed on the streets as well.

conservative　　entertainment　　gradually　　relaxed　　revolution

　1978年1月に始まったイラン革命は、イスラム革命とか民主主義革命とも言われた。1970年代は、世界的にソ連とアメリカの覇権争い、軍事紛争、政治的・経済的紛争が発生、継続していた。パフラヴィー王朝下のイランは、アメリカの援助を受け、脱イスラム化と世俗主義による近代化政策を取り続けていた。イスラム教勢力は弾圧を受け、排除されていたが、そこで亡命中であったホメイニーを精神的指導者であるイスラム教シーア派の法学者たちを支柱とする国民の勢力が政権を奪取した。1979年4月1日国民投票に基づいてイラン・イスラム共和国を樹立した。

　アメリカは、1980年4月にイランに国交断絶を通告し、経済制裁を発動した。イラン革命は世界情勢にも大きな影響を与え、イランとアメリカとの関係が険悪化したほか、中東の国々もイランと敵対するとともにイスラム主義が勢いを得るきっかけともなった。

　2018年11月アメリカがイランに対する経済制裁を再発動し、イラン国民は経済的苦境に立たされている。このアメリカの制裁をロシア、中国は非難し、国際社会でのアメリカの影響力低下を図る構えでいる。さらに、イランはイスラエル、サウジアラビアとも対立し、イラン情勢は益々緊迫化している。

Reading

57

Revolution at 40: Iranians Loosen Ideology's Grip on Daily Life

at 40：40歳の

In February of 1979, Tehran was in chaos. A cancer-stricken Mohammed Raza Pahlavi, the Western-backed autocrat, had gone into exile in mid-January, leaving behind a rickety regency council. On Feb. 1, Grand Ayatollah Ruhollah
5 Khomeini, the godfather of the revolution, returned from exile in Paris. And in the Iranian version of "Ten Days That Shook the World," street demonstrations raged until the government collapsed on Feb. 11.

58

Ecstatic Iranians danced in the streets, playing cat
10 and mouse with soldiers as lingering pro-government sharpshooters fired from the rooftops. Families joined in mass protests, as vigilantes ransacked liquor stores and people kissed the foreheads of turbaned clerics leading the revolution.

Forty years ago, Iranians swelled with pride, hope and
15 the expectation of a better future. But great, rapid change can leave deep and lasting wounds. There were lashings, hangings, amputations and mass imprisonment. Thousands of people died and hundreds of thousands left the country, some fleeing for their lives, never to return.

59
20 New rules were put in effect to forbid anything that might lead people astray and prevent them from ascending to a heavenly afterlife: strict controls on the media, which isolated Iranians from Western influences; an absolute segregation of the sexes in public places; compulsory head scarves
25 for women; bans on alcohol and musical instruments on television; rules forbidding women to ride bicycles. But over the years, as the early revolutionary fervor gave way for most people to a yearning for a more normal existence, the rules became negotiable.

30 It took time for the cumulative changes to reach a critical mass. When I first visited Iran as a young reporter, the 20th

---

Mohammed Raza Pahlavi：モハンマド・レザー・パフラヴィー《(1919-80)；イラン最後の皇帝；日本ではパーレビ国王と呼ばれた》

autocrat：専制君主

Grand Ayatollah Ruhollah Khomeini：大アッヤトゥラーのルニホッラー・ホメイニ師《アッヤトゥラーとはシーア派最高位ウラマー（知識人）の冠する称号で「神の徴」の意》

"Ten Days That Shook the World"：「世界を揺るがした10日間」《1917年のロシア十月革命》

raged：荒れ狂った

playing cat and mouse with 〜：〜と追いつ追われる

sharpshooters：狙撃手

vigilantes：自警団員、（犯罪者に）私的制裁を加える人

clerics：聖職者

swelled with 〜：〜でいっぱいだった

hangings：絞首刑

amputations：四肢切断

fleeing for their lives：命からがら逃げ出す

put in effect：実施された

astray：（人間として進むべき）道を外れて

segregation of the sexes：性差別

yearning for 〜：〜への憧れ、切望

normal existence：普通の生活

negotiable：守らないですむ

critical mass：臨界質量

anniversary of the revolution had just passed and the country was still living up to its revolutionary image. High rises were decorated with anti-American murals or portraits of the

35 martyrs of the 1980-88 war with Iraq.

In those days, it was inside people's houses that I saw a completely different Iran. Passing through a front door often meant stepping into a different reality, one where all the rules that applied on the streets would magically disappear.

40 Everyone — accountants, journalists, doctors, nurses — would enjoy weekend parties that were technically illegal.

But as the years progressed, the changes began to creep outdoors and become more noticeable.

Women now race through traffic riding bicycles, once

45 seen as improper. They can even be seen riding motorcycles.

Connections to the outside world — the internet, of course, but particularly satellite TV broadcasts that broke the veil of isolation — were critical drivers of change.

One day the police raided our apartment building and

50 destroyed the multitude of satellite dishes on the roof. The only one left was mine — as a journalist, I had special permission to have one. That evening about 20 female neighbors joined me in my living room to watch their favorite Turkish soap opera. By the next day, they all had new dishes.

55 The police have largely given up that fight, too. There are just too many dishes around.

The New York Times International Edition, February 11, 2019

---

living up to 〜：〜に従って行動する、生活する

High rises：高層ビル

martyrs：殉教者

it was 〜 that：強調構文

accountants：会計士

technically：厳密に言えば

drivers：推進力

satellite dishes：パラボラ・アンテナ

soap opera：（テレビ番組の）昼のメロドラマ、連続ホームドラマ《石鹸メーカーが番組スポンサーだったため》

Exercises

Multiple Choice

次の1～5の英文を完成させるために、a～dの中から最も適切なものを1つ選びなさい。

1. New rules were put into effect in Iran because
    a. people were joining in mall protests.
    b. drunken vigilantes were robbing liquor stores.
    c. people supported the turbaned clerics leading the revolution.
    d. of all of the above actions by the citizens.

2. The early revolutionary fervor
    a. continued for 40 years.
    b. created rules for citizens to assist in controlling "mob" mentality.
    c. was encouraged by Ayatollah Khomeini.
    d. encouraged citizens to play "cat and mouse" with the sharpshooters.

3. The main purpose of the rules was
    a. to keep Western influences away from the people.
    b. to let the people know the power of the Ayatollah.
    c. to allow the women to uncover their heads.
    d. to encourage the people to behave like Westerners.

4. As the years passed, the rules
    a. remained firmly in place to keep order.
    b. were enforced less strictly.
    c. were fully accepted by the people as their culture.
    d. prevented people from displaying anti-American banners.

5. The rules included
    a. separation of the sexes in public places.
    b. a ban on musical instruments and alcohol consumption.
    c. forbidding women to ride bicycles.
    d. all of the above restrictions.

本文の内容に合致するものに T（True）、合致しないものに F（False）をつけなさい。

(   ) **1.** The internet is partially responsible for rules being eased.

(   ) **2.** The author states that inside citizens' homes the rules for outside behavior were followed.

(   ) **3.** Nowadays rules have changed outside of the home.

(   ) **4.** Women are still not allowed to ride bicycles or motorcycles.

(   ) **5.** The author's satellite dish was not destroyed because journalists had special permission to have one.

Vocabulary

次の英文は、The New York Times に掲載された *In Iran's Crisis, the Middle Class Buckles in a Blink*『イランの危機で、中流階級は瞬く間に潰れた』の記事の一部です。下の語群から最も適切なものを 1 つ選び、（   ）内に記入しなさい。

Before their "downfall," as they call it, the Taymouris were the model (   )-class Iranian family, prosperous college-educated business owners who made enough (   ) to save for a down payment on their home. Now, they are a model for a different sort: the millions of middle-class Iranians who almost overnight have seen their lives (   ), dragged down by economic forces (   ) their control.

President Trump's decision to leave the (   ) deal, known formally as the Joint Comprehensive Plan of Action, or J.C.P.O.A., and to reimpose harsh economic sanctions prompted the other major (   ) disaster to befall Iran: a collapse in its currency, Mr. Salehi-Isfahani said. The rial lost about 70 percent against the (   ) before strengthening recently, but its rates are still fluctuating heavily.

Iran, with a population of about 80 million, has long had a large and (   ) middle class, covering roughly everyone from bus drivers to lawyers and doctors, and earning an average of $700 a month in local currency, according to government officials.

beyond	dollar	economic	middle
money	nuclear	shrink	thriving

● ケニアでは足が速いと身を滅ぼす

ケニアのエルドレットで練習に励むランナーたち　Photo: The New York Times ／ Redux ／アフロ

Before you read

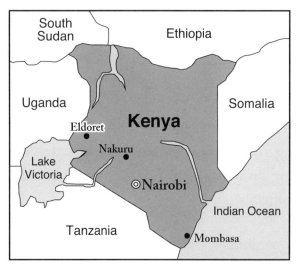

Republic of Kenya
ケニア共和国

面積　2,150,000km^2（日本の約5.7倍）
人口　49,700,000人
首都　ナイロビ
公用語　スワヒリ語　英語
民族　キクユ族　17.2%　／ ルヒヤ族　13.8%
　　　カレンジン族　12.9%　／ レオ族　10.5%
　　　カンバ族　10.1%　／ ソマリ族　6.2%
宗教　キリスト教・プロテスタント　47.7%
　　　　　　　　カトリック　23.5%
　　　その他のキリスト教　11.9%
　　　イスラム教　11.2%　／ 無宗教　2.4%
GDP　705億ドル
通貨　ケニア・シリング
政治　共和制
識字率　87.4%

次の１～５の語の説明として最も近いものをa～eから１つ選び、（　）内に記入しなさい。

1. toe （　） **a.** large number in a small area
2. concentration （　） **b.** widespread
3. peer （　） **c.** full
4. prevalent （　） **d.** stand behind
5. flush （　） **e.** person with similar background

Summary

　次の英文は記事の要約です。下の語群から最も適切な語を１つ選び、（　）内に記入しなさい。

62

　Kenyan runners, especially from the Eldoret area, have become (　　　　) for their (　　　　) records. Many earn enough money from running to give their families a (　　　　) life. But because of scams, corruption, or poor knowledge of finance, few of them benefit (　　　　). Some famous (　　　　) now live miserably.

long-distance　　long-term　　poverty-free
record-breakers　world-famous

　1963年にケニアは英連邦王国として独立し、翌年共和国が成立した。ジョモ・ケニヤッタが初代大統領に就任し、ケニアは経済成長を遂げた。資本主義体制を堅持し、東アフリカでは最も経済の発達した国になった。しかし、政情不安や政治の腐敗・非能率、貧富の差の増大という問題を抱え、国民には多難な生活が強いられてきている。

　ケニアのGDPの３割を農業が占めている。また労働力人口の約７割が農業に従事し、約８割が農業によって生計を立てている。工業化は、他のアフリカ諸国と比べると進んでいる。鉱物資源は種類、産出量とも少ないが、金の産出量が1.6トンに拡大している。

　５年前の貿易額は、輸出額51億6900万ドル、輸入額が120億9300万ドルで、70億ドル近くの貿易赤字がある。外貨の収入を価格不安定な資源輸出に頼ってきていて、ITなど産業の多角化を図っている。インド、中国、アラブ首長国連邦等が主要輸入先であるが、日本からの輸入額も９億ドル以上で、輸送機器が60%近くを占めている。

　ケニアには42の民族、60以上の言語が存在している。15歳以上の国民の識字率は87.4%である。スポーツでは陸上競技の長距離走の人気が高く、北京オリンピック男子マラソン金メダリストのサムエル・ワンジルがいる。

Reading

63

In Kenya, running can be a road to ruin

ruin：破滅

Ten years ago, in the Dutch port city of Rotterdam, Duncan Kibet lay spread-eagle on the pavement, attempting to process the record-setting run he had just completed and how it was about to change his life.

spread-eagle：大の字に

process ～：～を現像し焼き付ける《目的語は run と how 以下》

record-setting：新記録の

5 When he toed the starting line of the 29th Rotterdam Marathon that morning, April 5, 2009, he had been earning a living as an elite athlete for nearly a decade. But with a marathon personal best of only 2 hours 7 minutes 53 seconds, he was hardly a household name in Kenya, home to the 10 world's greatest concentration of distance running talent. Then he ran a 2:04:27, nearly three and a half minutes faster, making him Kenya's national record-holder and the second fastest marathoner in history.

household name：よく知られている人物

64

The win was worth big money for Kibet, who, like most of 15 his running peers, had grown up poor.

worth big money：大金に相当する

He bought a house for his mother in Eldoret, the de facto Kenyan running capital, and a Toyota Hilux truck. There were school fees for various relatives and contributions to a home for orphans. He bought Italian suits and had baseball caps and 20 shirts shipped from the United States.

Eldoret：エルドレット《ケニア中部の高原地帯、リフトバレー州にある都市》

de facto：事実上の

contributions to ～：～への献金

A groin injury kept him from finishing marathons in Berlin and London. His fitness waned, and two years after his Rotterdam triumph, he was essentially broke and out of work.

groin：鼠径部（脚の付け根）

fitness：(肉体の) 調子の良さ

broke：無一文の

Here in the Rift Valley, the high-altitude region that is 25 home to the vast majority of Kenya's elite athletes, the belief in running as an escape from poverty remains prevalent, but few among the thousands of young athletes who flock to training camps each year ever make a living from running.

prevalent：広く行き渡っている

Benjamin Limo, the 2005 world champion in the 30 5,000 meters and a former Kenyan representative to the International Association of Athletics Federations, track and field's governing body, estimated that only 25 percent

International Association of Athletics Federations：国際陸上競技連盟

track and field's governing body：陸上競技の統括団体

of the country's former top-level athletes were living in a "sustainable" manner.

35　　Kenyan champions often have large networks of family to support. Most have little schooling, some are barely literate and few have any experience managing money. A sudden infusion of cash, veteran athletes said, can distract from training and lead to careless spending.

40　　Eldoret, like most cities in Kenya, is home to its share of con artists, and athletes flush with cash are easy targets. A common scam involves the sale of fake land titles. In 2011, in a financial pinch, Kibet sold the house he had purchased after Rotterdam. The buyer, he claimed, paid him only half
45 the value, but gave him the title to another, smaller property. That deal turned out to be a fraud.

　　Athletes say the same about Athletics Kenya, the national federation that oversees the sport on behalf of the Kenyan government. It has gotten mixed up in a series of scandals,
50 including the embezzlement of payments from Nike by former top officials. As an Athletics Kenya representative, Limo proposed the creation of a pension plan to assist athletes struggling in retirement. He failed to gain support.

The New York Times International Edition, April 23, 2019.

"sustainable" manner：「持続可能な」態様

support 〜：〜を扶養する
literate：読み書きが出来る
managing money：資産管理
infusion：注入
distract from 〜：〜から遠ざける
share of con artists：詐欺師の分け前
flush with 〜：〜を豊富に持った
scam：（信用）詐欺
land titles：土地所有権

property：不動産物件
fraud：詐欺（ペテン）行為
Athletics Kenya：ケニア陸上競技連盟
on behalf of 〜：〜の代わりに
mixed up in 〜：〜に手を染めた
embezzlement：着服、使い込み
top officials：幹部
pension plan：年金計画（制度）
struggling in 〜：〜で苦労する

Exercises

Multiple Choice

次の1～4の英文を完成させ、5の質問に答えるために、a～dの中から最も適切なものを1つ選びなさい。

1. When Duncan Kibet ran a record setting marathon,

   a. he was hoping to improve his life by winning the race and obtaining the prize money.
   b. his name was not well known in Kenya.
   c. it made him the second fastest marathoner in history.
   d. all of the above situations were true.

2. This article explains that

   a. winning a race may bring cash as well as personal satisfaction.
   b. winning one race will bring you enough money to retire forever.
   c. an athlete does not need to heal before running another race.
   d. an athlete needs to be literate.

3. The race that Kibet won was held in

   a. the Rift Valley, Kenya.
   b. Berlin, Germany.
   c. Rotterdam, Netherlands.
   d. London, Great Britain.

4. A disappointing fact is that

   a. marathoners make enough money to live in the Rift Valley.
   b. Athletics Kenya has been accused of embezzlement.
   c. a pension plan for athletes in retirement was supported.
   d. Athletics Kenya does not represent the government.

5. What percentage of athletes are living "financially comfortable lives" as a result of winning races?

   a. 10%.   **c.** 20%.
   b. 15%.   **d.** 25%.

本文の内容に合致するものに T（True）、合致しないものに F（False）をつけなさい。

(   )   **1.**   Kibet was swindled out of his home in Rotterdam by a con man.

(   )   **2.**   Most athletes make no effort to support their families, even though they may have won their marathons.

(   )   **3.**   Kibet won in the Berlin marathon race.

(   )   **4.**   After winning the Rotterdam marathon, Kibet lay on the ground at the finish line because of his injury.

(   )   **5.**   Eldoret has a high number of con men looking for "victims" to take their money in some way.

Vocabulary

次の 1 〜 10 は、日本語の「走る」を使った語句です。日本文に合わせて、（   ）内に最も適切な動詞を下の語群から 1 つ選び、必要があれば適当な形に直して記入しなさい。

1. プログラムに沿って走るだけでいいです。
You just have to (   ) the program

2. 公園を毎朝ゆっくり走っている。
I (   ) in the park every morning

3. 彼はすぐ私利私欲に走る。
He (   ) his own self-interest

4. この列車は、現在時速20km だけで走っている。
This train is (   ) along at just 20 kilometers per hour.

5. 背中に痛みが走った。
Pain (   ) up my back.

6. 彼は自暴自棄となり、飲酒に走った。
In his desperation, he (   ) to drink.

7. 彼は、大儲けを当て込んで犯行に走った。
He (   ) the crime in expectation of gaining a large profit.

8. 彼女は極端に走った。
She (   ) to extremes.

9. 私はヘビを見るだけでムシズが走る。
I (   ) the mere sight of snakes.

10. 走っている車から飛び降りた。
He jumped out of a (   ) car.

commit	crawl	follow	go	hate
jog	move	pursue	shoot	turn

Unit **12**

●高層アパート崩壊でロシアの背骨にひずみが判明

ロシアの地方都市で老朽化した高層アパートが崩壊

Photo: AP ／アフロ

Before you read

Russian Federation　ロシア連邦
1991年12月25日ソ連崩壊によりソビエト連邦
の継承国として独立

面積　17,098,246km^2（日本の約45倍）
首都・最大都市　モスクワ
公用語　ロシア語
人口　146,804,400人
民族　スラブ人　82.7%　／テュルク系　8.7%
　　　コーカサス系　3.7%　／ウラル系　1.6%
宗教　ロシア正教会　63%
　　　その他のキリスト教　4.5%
　　　イスラム教　6.6%　／仏教　0.5%
　　　ユダヤ教　0.6%
識字率　99.7%
GDP　1兆2,807億ドル
通貨　ロシア・ルーブル
政治　共和制・連邦制

Words and Phrases

次の1～5の語の説明として最も近いものをa～eから1つ選び、（　）内に記入しなさい。

1. flee　　　　　　（　　）　a. remote areas
2. stir　　　　　　（　　）　b. money store
3. coffer　　　　　（　　）　c. without injury
4. hinterland　　　（　　）　d. arouse or provoke
5. unscathed　　　（　　）　e. escape

Summary

次の英文は記事の要約です。下の語群から最も適切な語を1つ選び、（　）内に記入しなさい。

68

　　President Putin favors military expansion (　　　　　) investment in his country's aging infrastructure. Russia has (　　　　) maintained its international political position, but many of its people continue to live in poor (　　　　). Yet Putin himself (　　　　) popular, even (　　　　　) Russians who have suffered building collapses.

> among　　conditions　　consequently　　over　　remains

　　ロシアは、社会主義体制から市場経済への移行を果たしたことで、社会内部の経済格差が拡大した。その後、2008年のリーマンショックによる世界金融危機、クリミア併合後の欧米による経済制裁、原油価格の下落、シリア内戦への介入等で景気が悪化を受け、ロシアでは貧富の格差が益々広がっている。ルーブルの暴落に伴いインフレが加速し、生活水準の低下で小売売上高は落ち込み、実質所得が2018年までに5年連続で減り、経済苦境が続いている。

　　さらに、ロシアの地域格差が著しく拡大している。モスクワやサンクトペテルブルクを中心とする大都市と天然資源の豊富な地域には多大な恩恵がもたらされているが、それ以外の地域には不況が続いている。寒冷地域である極東やシベリアでは、インフラ整備が遅れているため人口流出が続いていて、地域経済の停滞を招いている。

　　2018年のアメリカの調査会社ギャラップによると、ロシアの15歳から29歳の若者の44%が外国へ移住したいと希望していることが明らかになった。移住希望先は、ドイツの15%、アメリカの12%、日本が5%で3位に入った。

Reading

69

Strain on Russia's backbone

| Deadly high-rise collapse puts focus on hardships faced by ordinary people |

Strain：ひずみ

A loud bang startled Anna P. Timofeyeva awake. She reached for the light, but the electricity had gone out. In the dark, she and her husband quickly dressed their 2-year-old son and prepared to flee.

70

5 The explosion that caused the collapse of Mrs. Timofeyeva's high-rise building a week ago in the city of Magnitogorsk in southern Russia killed 39 people and initially stirred fears of terrorism. But the authorities have since blamed what to the average Russian is an even greater danger: crumbling

10 infrastructure and buildings, including Soviet-era apartment blocks.

Magnitogorsk：マグニトゴルスク《ロシア連邦チェリャビンスク州の都市；ウラル山脈南部の東麓に位置》

blamed 〜：〜のせいにした

to 〜：〜にとって《挿入で blamed what is … となる》

For a decade or more, as oil revenues have swelled its coffers, the Kremlin has poured resources into its armed forces, developing new weapons, upgrading its nuclear stockpile and

15 overhauling and professionalizing its army, navy and military intelligence agency.

revenues：収益金

coffers：財源

Kremlin：ロシア政府《旧ロシア帝国の宮殿名》

intelligence agency：情報機関

71

The results — whether military interventions in Syria and Ukraine or meddling in politics in Europe or the United States — have buttressed President Vladimir V. Putin's drive

20 to restore Russia to major-power status.

interventions：介入

meddling in 〜：〜に干渉する

drive：意欲

Yet, the apartment collapse and an earlier, highly unpopular cut in state pensions serve as a reminder of the lingering hardships that ordinary Russians are asked to endure, particularly those who live in the country's hinterlands.

state pensions：国家恩給

serve as 〜：〜として働く

hinterland：奥地、辺境

25 In the case of the accident in Magnitogorsk, what was said to have been a natural gas explosion sheared off a section of the building, flattening dozens of apartments but leaving Mrs. Timofeyeva's unscathed. "We were lucky," she said.

sheared off 〜：〜を削り取った

Magnitogorsk — which means Magnetic Mountain and

30 is named for nearby iron-ore deposits so large that they are

deposits：鉱脈

said to distort compass readings — is a city whose very name has long been redolent of the hardships of Russia's industrial backwaters. It was conjured from the empty steppe by decree of Joseph Stalin and intended as a model communist city, populated by enthusiastic volunteers known as shock workers. Its roughly 415,000 residents today earn average monthly wages of $360.

Today, most residents live in tenement-style concrete high-rises like the one that collapsed last week on Karl Marx Street. Built in 1973 and housing about 1,300 people, it was of a type of mass-produced, utilitarian housing seen throughout the former Eastern Bloc.

Several residents praised Mr. Putin for visiting within a day of the catastrophe, and they directed their anger at the local authorities.

Vladimir Y. Vorontsov, 71, a retired steelworker whose son died, showed up seething for a meeting with the Chelyabinsk region governor. "My son was crushed to death, and these clowns are still sitting here," he said of the bureaucrats. "They receive money and do nothing."

The authorities are to pay compensation of one million rubles, or about $14,800, to the families of those who died. Renters who lost apartments will get 50,000 rubles, or about $740, to compensate for personal items.

By week's end, heartbroken families and friends had begun to lay loved ones to rest in Magnitogorsk's Left Bank Cemetery, where the headstones were heaped in snow.

The New York Times International Edition, January 7, 2019

distort compass readings：方位磁石の読み取りを歪める

redolent of ～：～を暗示する

decree：命令

Joseph Stalin：ヨシフ・スターリン《(1878-1953)；ソ連の第2代最高指導者》

shock workers：(旧ソ連の)特別作業隊

tenement-style：共同住宅（アパート）様式の

Eastern Bloc：東欧 (共産)圏

catastrophe：大惨事

steelworker：製鋼工

seething：(怒りで) 煮えくりかえりながら

region governor：州知事

clowns：役立たず（な者たち）

bureaucrats：役人

compensation：補償金

Renters：借家人

Left Bank Cemetery：ウラル川東岸共同墓地

headstones were heaped in snow：墓石には雪が降り積もっていた

Exercises

Multiple Choice

次の１の質問に答え、２〜５の英文を完成させるために、 a 〜 d の中から最も適切なもの
を１つ選びなさい。

1. Who established this "perfect Communist city"?

    a. Vladimir Putin.   **c.** Joseph Stalin.

    b. Nikita Khrushchev.   **d.** Karl Marx.

2. The high-rise building collapsed because of

    a. a gas leak.

    b. poor construction.

    c. rebuilding the infrastructure.

    d. the force of a magnetic mountain.

3. The Russian Government has poured its profits into

    a. rebuilding more up-to-date housing for Russian citizens.

    b. building its armed forces and upgrading its nuclear arsenal.

    c. increasing pensions for workers.

    d. continuing a program to interfere in U.S. politics.

4. The workers at Magnitogorsk earn

    a. 415 dollars a month.

    b. no pension.

    c. 740 dollars a month.

    d. 360 dollars a month.

5. Putin and the government decided to

    a. pay 740 dollars to citizens who lost relatives in the collapsed building.

    b. pay no money to the families of the dead, since it was an accident.

    c. give any family who lost a loved one 14,800 dollars for compensation.

    d. honor the dead by allowing them to be buried in the local cemetery.

本文の内容に合致するものに T（True）、合致しないものに F（False）をつけなさい。

(   ) **1.** Putin is trying to restore Russia to major power status.

(   ) **2.** The infrastructure of the housing for citizens is able to withstand explosions.

(   ) **3.** Putin visited the fallen building the day after the disaster.

(   ) **4.** Thirteen hundred people were killed in the gas explosion collapse.

(   ) **5.** The Russian people must endure many hardships.

Vocabulary

次の英文は、The New York Times International Edition に掲載された *Russia is clamping down on rap*『ロシアはラップを取り締まっている』の記事の一部です。下の語群から最も適切なものを１つ選び、(   ) 内に記入しなさい。

A culture war heats up with the (   ) of a popular performer for 'hooliganism'.　One of Russia's most high-profile (   ) is serving 12 days in jail in the latest culture war skirmish about what constitutes acceptable entertainment.

A provincial court in the southern city of Krasnodar sentenced the rapper, Dimitri Kuznetsov, 25, known as Husky, on Nov. 23 on charges of (   ) and of refusing to take a (   ) test, Russian news outlets reported.

The sentence is the latest in a series of confrontations pitting rappers against (   ) enforcement, local officials or vigilante groups who have pushed to (   ) down a musical genre that the authorities say promotes drug use, suicide and other social ills.

It comes amid a campaign by President Vladimir V. Putin and the Russian Orthodox Church to (   ) family values, with ambitious officials or groups often pushing initiatives that they apparently hope will (   ) the Kremlin's attention.

attract	hooliganism	jailing	law
medical	promote	rappers	shut

- フランス人　中国人によるぶどう園の名称変更に恐怖で縮み上がる

フランスで最も名高いワイン地方のボルドーで中国人がワイン醸造所を取得

Photo: The New York Times ／ Redux ／アフロ

Before you read

フランスワイン産地

Alsace　アルザス
Champagne　シャンパーニュ
The Loire Valley　ロワール
Bordeaux　ボルドー
Bourgogne　ブルゴーニュ
Jura et Savoie　ジュラ・サヴォア
The Rhone Valley　ローヌ
Provence et Corse
　プロヴァンス・コルシカ
Languedoc-Roussillon
　ラングドック・ルーション
Southwest　南西地方

Words and Phrases

次の１〜５の語の説明として最も近いものをa〜eから１つ選び、（　）内に記入しなさい。

1. cringe　　　　　（　　）　　　**a.** confusing or worrying

2. fabled　　　　　（　　）　　　**b.** historical and famous

3. contention　　　（　　）　　　**c.** access to cash

4. liquidity　　　　（　　）　　　**d.** feel uncomfortable

5. disconcerting　（　　）　　　**e.** belief

Summary

次の英文は記事の要約です。下の語群から最も適切な語を１つ選び、（　）内に記入しなさい。

（　　　　　　　）, the French do not name wineries and chateaus （　　　　　）
rabbits or antelopes. But increased Chinese （　　　　　） of Bordeaux's
famous vineyards has brought a slew of new names. Although some locals
do not like the changes, others welcome the （　　　　　） interest. Moreover,
foreigners have always been a part of Bordeaux's wine （　　　　　）.

after	commercial	industry	ownership	traditionally

　2019年２月にフランス２テレビ（国営テレビ局）は「フランスのワイナリーを購入した後に、ワイナリーの名前を変えるという中国のバイヤーの慣行は、フランスでは多くの論争を引き起こしている。フランスのワイン文化に対して"失礼"にあたると考える人がいる一方、改名は中国の企業家のマーケティング戦略に過ぎず、大騒ぎする必要はないと指摘する人もいる」と報じている。

　シャトー・ラルトーが、中国の「うさぎ皇帝」を意味するフランス語の「ラパン・アンペリアル Lapin Impérial」、シャトー・セニャックがチベットカモシカ「アンテロープ・チベタン Antilope Tibétain」に改名された。産地の歴史に由来せず、中国で売りさばくために変更し、ワインボトルに刻印されることに、フランスの映画作家のソレルス氏は「歴史の一部の消滅だ」と強く非難している。

　ボルドーの6000のブドウ園中、140が中国人に所有されている。中華思想による世界支配の一環ではないかと警鐘を鳴らす人もいる。

Reading

75

French cringe as Chinese rename vineyards

Bordeaux has welcomed the newcomers' money,
but fears for its traditions

The rabbit — the "Imperial Rabbit" — looks out quietly from the vineyard's sign, sandwiched among the familiar words "Great Wine of Bordeaux."

But there are no rabbits in this vineyard, imperial or
5   otherwise. Nor are there any "Golden Rabbits" or "Tibetan Antelopes" or even "Grand Antelopes" in the vineyards not far away.

76

That has not stopped a Chinese owner in one of France's most fabled wine regions from naming his newly acquired
10 chateaus after them — to more than a little consternation among tradition-bound French.

There is perhaps no place more synonymous with France and its tradition of fine wines than Bordeaux. The style of its long-aging, leathery blends of cabernet sauvignon and merlot,
15 to name just two, are sought after the world over.

Yet despite the protestations when it comes to the Chinese, this story of invasion is not necessarily a new one for the region on the southwest coast of France.

For centuries, Bordeaux has adapted to foreign money and
20 tastes, with a flexibility that belies the purists' contention that tradition is inviolable.

77

Bordeaux accommodated the English when it was under their domination in the 12th and 13th centuries, and the Dutch who drained its marshes in the 17th century.

25 It opened its cellars to the Germans during the Nazi occupation, and more recently it shifted its taste to accommodate the preferences of the California-influenced American wine critic Robert Parker.

Bordeaux goes where the money is. And the money is now
30 with the Chinese.

---

cringe：恐怖で縮み上がる

Bordeaux：ボルドー《フランス南西部のジロンド県にある都市；赤ワインの産地で有名》

"Tibetan Antelopes"：「チベット・アンテロープ」《ウシ科の動物で絶滅危機にある》

stopped ... from ...：〜が…するのを止めさせた

chateaus：シャトー《本来は「城」だが、ボルドー地方ではブドウの栽培から行う「ワイン醸造所」》

consternation：驚愕、狼狽

synonymous with 〜：〜と同義の

The style of its long-aging：《文頭に With を置くと分かりやすい。blends が主語で動詞は are》

leathery blends of 〜：〜をブレンドした滑らかな味わいのワイン

cabernet sauvignon：カベルネ・ソーヴィニヨン《赤ワイン用ブドウの品種》

merlot：メルロー《辛口赤ワイン用の黒ブドウの一種》

adapted to 〜：〜に適応した

belies 〜：〜を裏切る

drained 〜：〜の水を抜いた

cellars：地下貯蔵室

preferences：好み

"It's a good thing there are Chinese investors, most definitely. Because there are too many producers here, and there's too much wine," said Nan Hu, the director general of the Clos des Quatre Vents, the sumptuous property of a state-
35 owned energy and real estate conglomerate from China.

Indeed, not all French here are so put out.

One is Jean Pierre Amoreau, a celebrated maker of Bordeaux at Château Le Puy. Is he worried? "Not at all," he said.

40 The Chinese were helping a lot of owners who, because of high French inheritance taxes, often can't afford to pass their properties on to children, he argued.

"The Chinese have a lot of liquidity, so they are helping these owners have a decent retirement," he said. "And they are
45 helping to preserve the chateaus."

Jean-Marie Garde, a producer who heads the winemakers syndicate in the storied Pomerol district nearby, agreed, to a point.

"For the Chinese, we say, 'Why not?'" Mr. Garde said.
50 "They are present, but not that present."

Still, "We're all a little disconcerted by this name-changing," Mr. Garde said. "And what's a bit disconcerting, too, is that you never meet them," he said of the new Chinese proprietors.

55 Yet they have not been entirely invisible, either. It was startling, for some, to see the red Chinese flag floating above the Clos des Quatre Vents, within sight of the famous Château Margaux in the Médoc, maker of the highest ranked of all Bordeaux wines.

The New York Times International Edition, April 8, 2019

director general：社長

Clos des Quatre Vents：クロ・デ・カトル・ヴァン（四つの風のぶどう園）
property：不動産物件
put out：気を悪くする

Château Le Puy：シャトー・ルピュイ

inheritance taxes：(遺産) 相続税

liquidity：流動性
decent：見苦しくない、立派な

Jean-Marie Garde：ジャン・マリー・ガルド《シャトー・ムリネ・ラセールの現当主》
syndicate：団体
to a point：ある程度

that：それほど、そんなに

disconcerted：まごつく、当惑する

Château Margaux：シャトー・マルゴー《ボルドー・ワインの醸造元》
Médoc：メドック《ジロンド県内の地区名》

Exercises

Multiple Choice

次の１～５の英文を完成させるために、ａ～ｄの中から最も適切なものを１つ選びなさい。

1. The Chinese help the French by
   a. refusing to pay inheritance taxes.
   b. preserving the chateaus and wineries.
   c. taking excess wine from the French without paying for it.
   d. naming their chateaus after animals.

2. French winemakers have adapted to please
   a. the English in the 12th and 13th centuries.
   b. the Dutch in the 17th century.
   c. the Germans during the Nazi invasion of World War II.
   d. all of the above foreigners.

3. The Chinese investors and the French winemakers
   a. hardly meet each other.
   b. become close friends.
   c. agree to only order merlot wine.
   d. are annoyed that the Chinese hung their national flag at a French winery.

4. The French realize that
   a. they are unhappy to sell their wine.
   b. the Chinese have the means to invest in France.
   c. they have never been invaded by other countries before.
   d. Bordeaux wine is not well known beyond France.

5. The headline tells us that
   a. the French are upset to have their chateaus named after animals by the Chinese.
   b. the new names will attract more Chinese tours.
   c. the French are desperate for financial assistance.
   d. the French regret their decision to let the Chinese become involved in their wine business.

本文の内容に合致するものに T（True）、合致しないものに F（False）をつけなさい。

(　　) **1.** The Bordeaux area is on the southeast coast of France.

(　　) **2.** Cabernet sauvignon and merlot are perhaps the most popular of the Bordeaux wines.

(　　) **3.** Some French are happy to have the Chinese help to finance the wine business.

(　　) **4.** The red Chinese flag is not allowed by French law to fly over the vineyards in France.

(　　) **5.** Chinese financial liquidity is allowing some French to have a good retirement.

Vocabulary

次の英文は、The New York Times に掲載された *An Italian Luxury Brand Is Drawing Fire in China*『イタリアの有名ブランドが中国で非難されている』の記事の一部です。下の語群から最も適切なものを１つ選び、（　　）内に記入しなさい。

Instagram may be blocked in China, but it can still make waves there.

Dolce & Gabbana, the Italian luxury brand, found that out on Wednesday with stunning swiftness. It (　　　　) canceled a Shanghai fashion show it had been planning to hold that night as waves of online Chinese users (　　　　) Stefano Gabbana, one of the two designers of the fashion line, of being (　　　　). They pointed to private Instagram messages from Mr. Gabbana's account that the recipient posted publicly.

"We are very (　　　　) for any distress caused by these unauthorized posts," Dolce & Gabbana said on its Instagram account. "We have (　　　　) but respect for China and the people of China." "I love China and the Chinese (　　　　)," Mr. Gabbana said. "I'm so sorry for what happened."

The latest online flap features a young Chinese woman in a glittery red dress and dangling jewelry trying to eat a cannoli with (　　　　). The ad was meant to play on Italian and Chinese cultural (　　　　).

| abruptly | accused | chopsticks | culture |
| differences | nothing | racist | sorry |

● ブラックホールの初画像：光の墓場を覗き込む

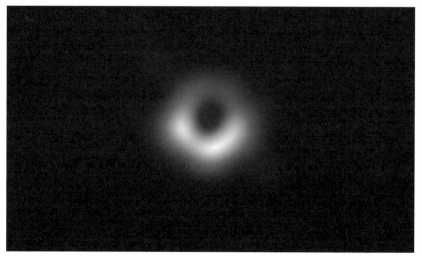

ブラックホールの「撮影」に初成功   Photo: Event Horizon Telescope ／ ZUMA Press ／アフロ

Before you read

1. What do you think the article will be about?

   この記事は何の話題についてだと思いますか？

2. What do you know about black holes?

   ブラックホールについては何を知っていますか？

次の１〜５の語の説明として最も近いものをa〜eから１つ選び、（　）内に記入しなさい。

1. peer　　　　　　　　（　）　　　a. coordinate
2. abyss　　　　　　　（　）　　　b. look closely
3. constellation　　　（　）　　　c. group of stars
4. quiver　　　　　　　（　）　　　d. deep and dark place
5. synchronize　　　　（　）　　　e. shake

次の英文は記事の要約です。下の語群から最も適切な語を１つ選び、（　）内に記入しなさい。

Even Einstein had (　　　　　　) about black holes, the astonishing phenomena he (　　　　　　) when developing the theory of general relativity. But a recent global collaboration has (　　　　　) their existence. Telescopes around the world have produced our first (　　　　　) of the Virgo black hole, 5000 light years (　　　　　　) and billions of times more massive than the sun.

away　　confirmed　　doubts　　images　　predicted

2019年４月、強い重力で光さえものみこむ謎の天体「ブラックホール」の撮影に、国立天文台や世界約80の研究機関による国際チームがついに成功した。1915年、アインシュタインが、重力に関する理論「一般相対性理論」を発表し、翌1916年にドイツの天文学者シュバルツシルトがこの一般相対性理論をもとに、ブラックホールの存在を推定した。

オレンジ色に輝くガスのリングの中央に開いた黒い穴をとらえ、この穴の中心に「巨大ブラックホール」が確実に存在することが証明された。地球から約5500万光年も離れた楕円銀河「M87」の中心部を高い解像度で捉えた。リングの直径は、約1000億km、ブラックホールの質量が「太陽の約65億倍」と特定されている。

ブラックホールは重力が強く、光さえも脱出できないため、観測は極めて困難だった。この世界初のブラックホール撮影は、ブラックホールの存在を証明できたこと、観測に新たな手段を得たこと、そして銀河の成り立ちを知る手がかりとなった。しかし、なぜ巨大ブラックホールができたのかは天文学最大の謎のひとつである。

Reading

81

Peering Into Light's Graveyard:
The First Image of a Black Hole

Astronomers announced on Wednesday that at last they had captured an image of the unobservable: a black hole, a cosmic abyss so deep and dense that not even light can escape it.

5   "We have seen what we thought was unseeable," said Shep Doeleman, an astronomer at the Harvard-Smithsonian Center for Astrophysics, and director of the effort to capture the image, during a Wednesday news conference in Washington, D.C.

82

10   To capture the image, astronomers reached across intergalactic space to Messier 87, or M87, a giant galaxy in the constellation Virgo. There, a black hole several billion times more massive than the sun is unleashing a violent jet of energy some 5,000 light-years into space.

15   The image offered a final, ringing affirmation of an idea so disturbing that even Einstein, from whose equations black holes emerged, was loath to accept it. If too much matter is crammed into one place, the cumulative force of gravity becomes overwhelming, and the place becomes an eternal 20 trap. Here, according to Einstein's theory, matter, space and time come to an end and vanish like a dream.

83

     The unveiling Wednesday took place almost exactly a century after images of stars askew in the heavens made Einstein famous and confirmed his theory of general relativity 25 as the law of the cosmos. That theory ascribes gravity to the warping of space and time by matter and energy, much as a mattress sags under a sleeper.

     General relativity led to a new conception of the cosmos, in which space-time could quiver, bend, rip, expand, swirl 30 like a mix-master and even disappear forever into the maw of a black hole.

Peering Into ～：～を覗き込む

Astronomers：天文学者

abyss：深淵

Harvard-Smithsonian Center for Astrophysics：ハーバード・スミソニアン天体物理学センター

director：代表

intergalactic：銀河間の

Messier 87：《1781年にシャルル・メシエに発見された》

constellation Virgo：乙女座

unleashing ～：～を解き放つ

some 5,000 light-years into space：約5,000光年の広さの宇宙に渡り

disturbing：困惑させる

equations：方程式

crammed into ～：～に詰め込まれた

cumulative force of gravity：累積的な重力

askew：歪んで（浮かんでいる）

theory of general relativity：一般相対性理論

ascribes ～ to …：～は…のせいだ

warping：ねじれ

mix-master：ミックスマスター《ビデオゲームの名称；モンスターを育て、合体させ、より強いモンスターを手に入れる》

maw：吸い込み口

84

To Einstein's surprise, the equations indicated that when too much matter or energy was concentrated in one place, space-time could collapse, trapping matter and light in perpetuity. He disliked that idea, but the consensus today is that the universe is speckled with black holes furiously consuming everything around them.

Nobody knows how such behemoths of nothingness could have been assembled. Monster runaway stars that collapsed and swallowed up their surroundings in the dawning years of the universe?

Nor do scientists know what ultimately happens to whatever falls into a black hole, nor what forces reign at the center, where, theoretically, the density approaches infinity and smoke pours from nature's computer.

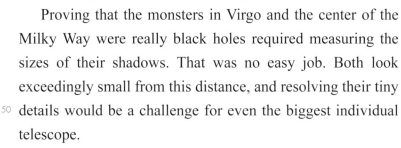
85

Proving that the monsters in Virgo and the center of the Milky Way were really black holes required measuring the sizes of their shadows. That was no easy job. Both look exceedingly small from this distance, and resolving their tiny details would be a challenge for even the biggest individual telescope.

In April 2017, the network of eight telescopes, including the South Pole Telescope, synchronized by atomic clocks, stared at the two targets off and on for 10 days.

The measurement also gave a firm estimate of the mass of the Virgo black hole: 6.5 billion solar masses.

The telescope network continues to grow. In April 2018, a telescope in Greenland was added to the collaboration.

The New York Times, April 11, 2019

in perpetuity：永久に

speckled with ～：～で染みが付いている
consuming ～：～を吸収する
behemoths：巨大なもの
runaway：暴走した

infinity：無限の数量

monsters：巨大ブラックホール
Milky Way：天の川銀河
shadows：暗部
resolving ～：～を解像すること

South Pole Telescope：南極点望遠鏡
atomic clocks：電波時計
off and on：断続的に

Exercises

Multiple Choice

次の1の質問に答え、2～5の英文を完成させるために、a～dの中から最も適切なもの
を1つ選びなさい。

1. How many telescopes does it take to measure the mass of the Virgo black
   hole?

   a. 9 telescopes.　　　　**c.** 8 telescopes.

   b. 7 telescopes.　　　　**d.** 10 telescopes.

2. The big news in astronomy is that

   a. there are no black holes in space.

   b. they captured an image of the black hole, a cosmic abyss.

   c. the black hole they found is smaller than the sun.

   d. there is only one black hole.

3. The cumulative force of gravity in a black hole

   a. becomes overwhelming.

   b. acts as a magnet trap.

   c. consumes matter, space, and time.

   d. does all of the above, as Einstein predicted.

4. The black hole in Virgo

   a. shoots a stream of energy 500 light years in space.

   b. shoots a foot of energy 5,000 light years in space.

   c. does not act as a magnetic force.

   d. is of medium size.

5. The astronomers

   a. knew what was at the center of a black hole.

   b. were puzzled as to how to do further exploration.

   c. continued their discovery by utilizing a large number of telescopes.

   d. took 10 hours to peer at the black hole.

True or False

本文の内容に合致するものに T（True）、合致しないものに F（False）をつけなさい。

( ) **1.** Einstein's findings were made 100 years before astronomers saw the black hole.

( ) **2.** Astronomers today believe that there are only a few black holes in space.

( ) **3.** The Virgo black hole is thought to be 6.5 billion solar masses.

( ) **4.** The author suggests that monster runaway stars collapsed and swallowed up their surroundings.

( ) **5.** The astronomers saw exactly what they had pictured before the exploration of the black hole.

Vocabulary

次のクロスワードパズルを、下の Across 横、Down 縦の英文説明を読んで、Unit 24 の記事から最も適切な語句を見つけ、□の中に１文字ずつ入れないさい。

ACROSS

3 agreement
5 extremely powerful
6 connected with the sun
8 tool to see distant things
9 invisible
10 100 years

DOWN

1 very big and heavy
2 a scientist who studies the stars
4 disappear
7 mathematical calculation

Unit 15

● ドイツ　高速道路で速度制限か？

自動車王国ドイツの自動車メーカーの配送タワー内光景　　　　Photo: AP／アフロ

Before you read

Federal Republic of Germany
ドイツ連邦共和国

面積　357,000km^2（日本の約94%）
首都・最大都市　ベルリン
公用語　ドイツ語
人口　82,450,000人
　　　ドイツ人　80.8%　／ヨーロッパ人　11.7%
　　　西アジア人　4.9%
　　　トルコ系　3.4%　／アラブ系　1.3%
宗教　キリスト教・カトリック　29.9%
　　　　　　　　　プロテスタント　28.9%
　　　イスラム教　2.6%
識字率　99%
GDP　3兆4,666億ドル（世界4位）
通貨　ユーロ
政体　連邦共和制

次の1～5の語句の説明として最も近いものをa～eから1つ選び、( )内に記入しなさい。

1. storied   ( )   a. controlled and orderly
2. aversion   ( )   b. famous
3. up there with   ( )   c. dislike
4. rational   ( )   d. at the same level as
5. regulated   ( )   e. reasoned and logical

Summary

次の英文は記事の要約です。下の語群から最も適切な語を1つ選び、( )内に記入しなさい。

86

 In a country where regulations even (   ) to umbrellas, one freedom Germans refuse to give up is the (   ) to drive at speed. Autobahn speed limits would be an (   ) way to reduce carbon emissions. But few people listen to the (   ). It seems Germans are crazy about speed just as Americans (   ) about firearms and Japanese about whales.

| argument | effective | extend | obsess | right |

 Autobahn アウトバーンは、自動車高速道路のことで、ドイツのアウトバーンは速度無制限道路として有名である。しかし、全区域が速度無制限ではなく、制限のある区域も存在する。混雑区間、合流分岐付近、急坂区間には時速100kmから130kmの制限速度が設定されている。速度無制限区間は路線全体の約50%と言われている。アウトバーンの総延長は約13,000kmである。法定最高速度はなく、推奨速度は時速130kmとされている。ドイツの法定最高速度ルールは簡単で、アウトバーン以外、市街地は時速50km, 住宅街・学校近辺は30km/h, それ以外は100km/hである。ドイツのアウトバーンは無料で、自動車燃料・保有への税金で道路建設と維持が行われている。
 1933年9月、首相となったヒトラーによる鍬入れ式が行われ、アウトバーンの建設が始まった。この建設工事の特徴は失業者を雇用し、失業者対策を行ったこと、コンクリート舗装を採用したことにある。「新しいドイツの建設」というナチ党の標榜する国民意識高揚に大きく寄与した。

Reading

87

Speed limit on the autobahn!

It seemed like a no-brainer: Lower Germany's embarrassingly high carbon emissions at no cost, and save some lives in the process.

But when a government-appointed commission in January
5 dared to float the idea of a speed limit on the autobahn, the country's storied highway network, it almost caused rioting.

As far as quasi-religious national obsessions go for large portions of a country's population, the German aversion to speed limits on the autobahn is up there with gun control in
10 America and whaling limits in Japan.

88

With few exceptions, like Afghanistan and the Isle of Man, there are highway speed limits essentially everywhere else in the world.

But this is Germany, the self-declared "auto nation," where
15 Karl Benz built the first automobile and where cars are not only the proudest export item but also a symbol of national identity.

Call it Germany's Wild West: The autobahn is the one place in a highly regulated society where no rule is the rule —
20 and that place is sacred.

89

Germany is woefully behind on meeting its 2020 climate goals, so the government appointed a group of experts to find ways to lower emissions in the transportation sector. A highway speed limit of 120 kilometers an hour, or 75 miles
25 per hour, could cover a fifth of the gap to reach the 2020 goals for the transportation sector, environmental experts say.

"Of all the individual measures, it is the one that would be the most impactful — and it costs nothing," said Dorothee Saar, of Deutsche Umwelthilfe, or Environmental Action Germany,
30 a nonprofit environmental organization that has lobbied for a speed limit.

"But when it comes to cars," Ms. Saar sighed, "the debate

autobahn：ドイツの高速道路

It seemed like a no-brainer：別に頭を悩ませる問題とは思えないが

carbon emissions：炭素排出量

at no cost：無料で

〜-appointed commission：〜によって設立された委員会

float the idea：アイデアを提案する

caused rioting：暴動を引き起こした

go for 〜：〜に襲いかかる

aversion to 〜：〜への嫌悪感

up there with 〜：〜と同じくらい重要である

gun control：銃規制

national identity：国民性

Wild West：（米国開拓時代の）西部地方

sacred：神聖不可侵な

cover 〜：〜を埋め合わせる

individual measures：個人が出来る方法

it is the one that would …：《強調構文》

Deutsche Umwelthilfe：ドイチェ・ウムヴェルトヒルフェ（ドイツ環境問題行動委員会）

lobbied for 〜：〜に賛成するよう議員に働きかけた

tends to become irrational."

90
35 "It's all about freedom," said John C. Kornblum, a former United States ambassador to Germany, who first arrived in Germany in the 1960s and has been living (and driving) here on and off ever since.

"In that sense it really is like gun control," Mr. Kornblum added, albeit with far fewer deaths. "All the rational arguments 40 are there, but there is barely any point in having a rational debate."

Mr. Kornblum, the former ambassador, remembered taking terrified visiting American diplomats for a drive. "The first reaction is to start screaming, 'We're going to die!'" he 45 said.

91
Or as the actor Tom Hanks once put it: "No matter how fast you drive in Germany, someone is driving faster than you."

Off the autobahn, Germany remains rife with rules. Some 50 local authorities even dictate the color of umbrellas.

"Germany is terribly regulated, for reasons which have to do with the past, with a fear of uncertainty, a fear of being overwhelmed," Mr. Kornblum said. "But then people look for their little spaces of freedom, and the autobahn is one of 55 them."

And speeding isn't the only freedom the autobahn offers. Driving naked in Germany is legal, too. But if you get out of the car nude, you face a $45 fine.

The New York Times International Edition, February 6, 2019

irrational：非理性的な

It's all about freedom：全ては自由の問題だ

albeit 〜：〜ではあるが

point in 〜：〜という考え

terrified：恐がりの

put it：言った

rife with 〜：〜で溢れている

dictate 〜：〜を指示する、命令する

have to do with 〜：〜と関係する

uncertainty：不確実性

legal：合法の、適法の

fine：罰金

Exercises

Multiple Choice
次の１〜５の英文を完成させるために、ａ〜ｄの中から最も適切なものを１つ選びなさい。

1. The author compares lowering the speed limit on the German autobahn to
   a. gun control in the USA.
   b. issues that are too emotional for people to discuss coolly.
   c. whaling limits in Japan.
   d. all of the above restrictions.

2. The well-known German export discussed in this article is
   a. beer.   c. cameras.
   b. automobiles.   d. sausages.

3. Germany has
   a. very few rules citizens must follow.
   b. many rules to follow except autobahn speed.
   c. a tendency to reassure first-time foreign drivers on the autobahn.
   d. an affinity with the Isle of Man because of strict speed limits.

4. The reason that officials are contemplating putting a speed limit on the autobahn is
   a. to lower the carbon emission numbers.
   b. to reduce a problem at little cost to the government.
   c. to lower the death and injury rates for drivers and passengers.
   d. to be found in all of the above statements.

5. One surprising thing is that the autobahn allows
   a. drivers of all ages.
   b. you to drive while you are nude.
   c. someone to drive faster than you.
   d. foreign diplomats to drive.

本文の内容に合致するものに T（True）、合致しないものに F（False）をつけなさい。

(   )   **1.**   A former Ambassador from the U. S. seems to enjoy driving on the autobahn.

(   )   **2.**   If you get out of your car naked, you receive a ticket.

(   )   **3.**   The carbon emissions are not of real concern to the government.

(   )   **4.**   Germany is definitely going to adopt a speed limit on the autobahn.

(   )   **5.**   German citizens might feel overwhelmed by rules in society but feel some freedom on the autobahn

Vocabulary

次の 1 〜 10 は、日本語の「出す」を使った語句です。日本文に合わせて、下の語群から最も適切なものを 1 つ選び、（   ）内に記入しなさい。

1.	スピードを出す	( )	speed
2.	優秀な学者を世に出す	( )	out excellent scientists
3.	強い匂いを出す	( )	off a strong smell
4.	ゴミを出す	( )	out the garbage
5.	論文を出す	( )	the paper
6.	コーヒーを出す	( )	coffee
7.	本を出す	( )	a book
8.	命令を出す	( )	commands
9.	返事を出す	( )	an answer
10.	テーブルに金メダルを出す	( )	a gold medal on the table

display	give	increase	issue	publish
put	send	serve	submit	turn

15章版：ニュースメディアの英語

――演習と解説2020年度版――

検印 省略	©2020年 1 月31日　初 版 発 行

編著者	高橋　優身
	伊藤　典子
	Richard　Powell
発行者	原　　雅久
発行所	株式会社朝日出版社

101-0065　東京都千代田区西神田3-3-5
電話（03）3239-0271
FAX（03）3239-0479
e-mail: text-e@asahipress.com
振替口座　00140-2-46008
組版・製版／信毎書籍印刷株式会社

乱丁，落丁本はお取り替えいたします
ISBN 978-4-255-15655-2 C1082

ちょっと手ごわい、でも効果絶大!
最強のリスニング強化マガジン

CNN ENGLISH EXPRESS

CNNライブ収録CD付き　毎月6日発売　定価（本体1,148円＋税）

実売No.1英語学習誌

定期購読をお申し込みの方には
本誌1号分無料ほか、特典多数。
詳しくは下記ホームページへ。

英語が楽しく続けられる!

重大事件から日常のおもしろネタ、
スターや著名人のインタビューなど、
CNNの多彩なニュースを
生の音声とともにお届けします。
3段階ステップアップ方式で
初めて学習する方も安心。
どなたでも楽しく続けられて
実践的な英語力が身につきます。

資格試験の強い味方!

ニュース英語に慣れれば、TOEIC®テストや英検の
リスニング問題も楽に聞き取れるようになります。

CNN ENGLISH EXPRESS ホームページ

英語学習に役立つコンテンツが満載!

[本誌のホームページ] https://ee.asahipress.com/
[編集部のTwitter] https://twitter.com/asahipress_ee

朝日出版社 〒101-0065 東京都千代田区西神田 3-3-5　TEL 03-3263-3321

世界標準の英語ニュースが だれでも聞き取れるようになる!

CNN ニュース・リスニング 2019[秋冬]

CD・MP3・対訳付き　A5判　定価(本体1,000円＋税)

1本30秒だから、聞きやすい!

- ●キム・カーダシアン、日本文化を盗用!?
- ●禁断の実験! 猿の脳に人間の遺伝子を移植
- ●スマホいじりで若者の頭にツノが生えた?…など

ご注文はこちら

朝日出版社 〒101-0065 東京都千代田区西神田 3-3-5　TEL 03-3263-3321

音声アプリ＋動画で、どんどん聞き取れる！

初級者からの
ニュース・リスニング

CNN Student News ▶
2019［夏秋］

A5判 定価（本体1,200円＋税）

🎧 CD付き │ 🔊 MP3 ＋ 📱 電子書籍版 ＋ 🖥 映像付き［オンライン提供］

● レベル別に2種類の速度の音声を収録
● ニュース動画を字幕あり/なしで視聴できる

ご注文はこちら

朝日出版社 〒101-0065 東京都千代田区西神田 3-3-5 TEL 03-3263-3321